New

and other

A manua

Stephen Bell, Pet

CORNWALL COUNTY COUNCIL
LIBRARIES AND ARTS DEPARTMENT
Education Library Services

Cambridge University Press

Cambridge

New York   Port Chester   Melbourne   Sydney

Published by the Press Syndicate of the University of Cambridge
The Pitt Building, Trumpington Street, Cambridge CB2 1RP
40 West 20th Street, New York, NY 10011, USA
10 Stamford Road, Oakleigh, Melbourne 3166, Australia

© Cambridge University Press 1989

First published 1989
Third printing 1990

Printed in Great Britain at the University Press, Cambridge

British Library cataloguing in publication data
Bell, Stephen
New York Cop and other investigations:
a manual for teachers.
1. Mathematics – For schools
I. Title   II. Brown, Peter   III. Buckley, Steven
510

ISBN 0 521 35864 7

UPS

No permission is required for duplication of the worksheets in this book within the school or college for which it was bought.

Contents

Introduction	**page** 4
Classroom usage	5
Assessment	7
Flow chart	15

Investigations

Hopping mad	16
Colour by number	18
Petfood pile	20
Stairs	24
Julius Squarius	28
Foxed	30
Noughts and crosses	32
A series of sums	34
The paperboy's problem	37
Number walls	41
Door numbers	45
Crossed lines	48
Rectangle mania	51
Hectic hockey	55
Chequered flags	59
Cutting corners	62
A cube investigation	66
Around the garden	70
Areas and perimeters	74
Brighouse market	77
New York Cop	81
Sheep dip	86
Pins in rectangles	89
Masters for walls, squares and spotty papers	93

Introduction

The introduction of the GCSE examinations has meant that all mathematics teachers have had to rethink their teaching of several subject areas. Perhaps the most important change has been the introduction of investigational work, the importance of which is highlighted in the Cockcroft Report.

Para 250 The idea of investigation is fundamental both to the study of mathematics itself and also to the ways in which mathematics can be used to extend knowledge and to solve problems in very many fields.

The teacher will find investigational work particularly important for several reasons. Firstly, it promotes inventiveness of thought and helps pupils to be logical and systematic in their approach to problem solving. Secondly, it gives pupils the opportunity to develop both oral and written skills. Variety can be added to the lessons not only by the more open nature of investigational work but also by the differences between the investigations themselves. Algebra becomes more purposeful in the eyes of the pupils. It also gives the less able pupils an opportunity to tackle algebraic techniques without the formalised structure being taught directly. At the other end of the ability range the more able are given scope to extend their work in a direction of their own chosing because of the openness of the work.

There are other books available which give course material for investigational work. We feel that some of the starting points are too abstract with the consequent lack of motivation. In other cases the opening descriptions have been either too complex or too vague, particularly for pupils new to this area of work. Most pupils need to see clear objectives if they are to make a success of problem solving.

In this book we have tried to give the investigations clear objectives and where possible they have been set in 'concrete' situations. The investigations have been written in a structured way in an attempt to promote a greater understanding of the problem. This is helpful to both pupil and teacher. It gives the pupil an opportunity to learn the techniques required for efficient problem solving and helps to develop report writing skills. The teacher is able to see where the investigation is going and then adapt and develop it accordingly.

It is most important that the teacher should not present all the investigations in this structured way so that pupils have freedom to develop their own style. As pupils gain confidence more open investigations should be set so that they may become true problem solvers. Examples of more open starting points are given in the book. The more structured approach can then be used as a source of hints to be used in response to pupils' questions. Suggestions for classroom use are included in the solution section.

We do not expect all pupils to complete all the investigations fully. It is appropriate for some pupils to complete only the first few sections, while the more able and enthusiastic should be encouraged to extend the problem to other fields.

Classroom usage

Pupils new to investigational work tend to see the work as either silly or too difficult. Generally this is because they cannot see a simple solution to the problem, that is it does not fit in with their mathematical experience.

Most pupils are used to answering a simple applied question like 'Jim gives his three children 27 stamps to share between them. How many stamps do they each receive?' or questions where they have to input certain known (learned) information, e.g.

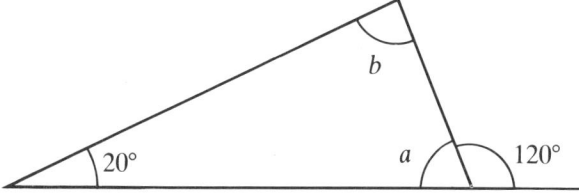

Calculate angles a and b.

There are certain procedures that are common to many investigations so that the approach to the solution of a problem is as important as the result itself. Investigational work requires pupils to extract their own information from a situation new to them and then to gather together, organise and summarise this information. From this patterns have to be formed which can then be extended to more complicated situations which would normally be unmanageable. Later a generalisation is made which is usually in some kind of algebraic form (although not necessarily using standard algebraic techniques). To do this work pupils may have to simplify the initial problem by limiting its scope or by adding constraints. To many pupils the task appears daunting; however, once the initial insecurity has been overcome many pupils tend to enjoy the freedom of the work and they are able to apply their knowledge and mathematical experiences more widely.

The way in which this kind of material is taught is markedly different from the more traditional classroom activities. Pupils have to learn to look further than simply finding the answer, while teachers have to see their role less as the provider of all knowledge but more as an experienced adviser. The investigations in this book have been written in a structured way and have been written in 'realistic' situations to help the pupils to transfer to this new way of thinking. In the teacher's notes an alternative form of the same question has been outlined which has been set in a much more open style. These are suggestions of how to present the same question to more experienced pupils; you will note that these have been written in varying degrees of 'openness'.

When introducing investigational work it is recommended that the pupils initially work in groups (three or four pupils in each group is probably the optimum size) with all the groups doing the same task. Group work gives pupils confidence to express ideas and they are less likely to become 'stuck' because of the interchange of ideas between members of the group. If all groups are doing the same investigation there can be a transfer of ideas from one group to another both formally and informally. Once pupils become familiar with investigational techniques it is advisable that they move on to individual work, although it is recommended that group work is not abandoned entirely. As the pupil's confidence and experience increases more open investigations can be introduced. An example of a more open version is given with every structured question. The teacher will have to judge when these changes should best be made, bearing in mind the stage of development of the class.

In common with most aspects of mathematics, investigational work becomes easier with practice. However, it is the problem solving techniques that are improved rather than a greater knowledge of the stock of questions.

Another major change in some classrooms will be the increase in oral work. The teacher will be working with small groups or with individual pupils. Discussion is valuable because pupils will have different ideas about a problem. Ideas will be exchanged, tested and consolidated through discussion with other pupils and the teacher. Pupils must feel confident to ask questions. It is important that nothing is dismissed as being wrong. All kinds of ideas will come from the pupils, many of which may not have been considered by the teacher. It is easy to overlook an original or valid solution merely because it is different from the solution given in this book. All ideas will show something about the way the pupil is thinking. The classroom may well become a much noisier place because of the enthusiasm generated by the work!

In some investigations pupils may not find the solution that the teacher was looking for or not be able to complete the investigation. This does not mean the work is of no value; just working through an investigation is of some use. It may be tempting to lead pupils to an answer, but this should be avoided whenever possible. There are two main reasons why pupils cannot make progress with an investigation. The first is that pupils do not organise their results in an orderly way or may not check their results for errors and so they try to draw conclusions from incorrect information. The other reason is that pupils try to generalise too early or set their own unrealistic constraints. Pupils should be encouraged to work from simple cases and build up their information systematically. They must always check their results and any assumptions made. Rules need to be tested with data to determine their validity.

It is important that the work set is suitable for the ability of the pupil – do not overload or present a totally unrealistic problem. An age/ability chart is given for each investigation. This should help the teacher to identify which piece of work is suitable. It is included as a general guide because different pupils will be able to benefit from the work to a greater or less extent depending on their previous experience. It is possible that some 14 to 16 year old pupils below the 40th percentile will be able to gain valuable experience from selected parts of the level 1 investigations (see the flowchart on page 15).

Ability	100–	80–	60–40
Age 13	–	–	–
14	12	6	–
15/16	/	Ext	12

The above age/ability chart may be interpreted as follows. A 14 year old pupil in the 60 to 40 percentile range should not be presented with the investigation. A 14 year old in the 80 to 61 percentile range should only be presented with work up to question 6. A 15 to 16 year old in the 80 to 61 percentile range should be able to complete the investigation and do some extension work. A 15 to 16 year old in the 100 to 81 percentile range will find the whole investigation too easy. The age/ability chart refers to the structured questions only since work set in an open context is more difficult to understand and answer. Pupils can often benefit from answering an open question which they have previously attempted in its structured form. Ideas for extension work are included in the notes but pupils should be encouraged to think of their own.

A teacher must avoid setting unrealistic time limits on an investigation. Shorter investigations can be completed within a single lesson. For a larger piece of work it may be necessary to start in class, so that problems of understanding can be ironed out, and to complete the investigation for homework. Pupils can then spend as much time as they think necessary. Do not let an investigation drag on too long expecting more and more to be found, because the project will lose its interest.

At the end of an investigation it is recommended that pupils write a 'report' of their findings. This should include examples of the work produced, tables, summaries and generalisations including any limitations and exceptions. An explanation of the result is important. If an investigation has been completed as a group exercise the report gives the teacher the opportunity to assess the understanding of the individual pupils within the group. It is advisable to start with one or two group reports before moving on to individuals writing their own reports.

Pupils will benefit from the teacher leading a class discussion after the work has been assessed either formally or informally. This discussion should be used to consolidate the objectives of the investigation whilst pointing out particular interesting ideas produced by the pupils. The underlying principles of the piece of work should be restated to reinforce the use of any techniques employed.

Assessment

The aim of assessment in this context is to produce a measure of a pupil's knowledge and ability to apply mathematical skills. If carefully undertaken it should give both the teacher and the pupil an idea of how well a piece of work has been tackled; it should reward the pupils for their effort; and it should also allow the teacher to identify areas of weakness that can be consolidated in later lessons.

Assessment in all areas of mathematics is difficult to do accurately and this is particularly true with investigations. In a simple Pythagoras question, for example, three marks may be awarded: one mark for recognising a Pythagoras question, one mark for stating the formula correctly and one mark for a correct solution. It is relatively easy to award marks for individual pupil's answers and to compare pupils' understanding of the question. In investigational work pupils will tackle and present answers to problems in completely different ways. The problem of assessing the relative merits of different pieces of work is to find and reward that which shows the most insight.

In all reports written by pupils there are several points which the teacher must assess.

1 Basic examples that are correct

In investigations pupils must work out simple, correct examples to establish a firm basis for later assumptions and hypotheses.

2 An ordered approach to these examples

Pupils need to build up their examples in a systematic way to ensure that account is taken of all eventualities and to avoid repeating work. An orderly approach will enable relationships to be spotted more easily.

3 Summarising the findings

This will usually take the form of a table of findings. The tabulation, or summarisation in some other form, of relevant information usually makes the spotting of relationships and patterns easier.

4 Spotting patterns in the results

This is an important skill because it allows pupils to generate answers to questions that are too difficult or cumbersome to find using other methods. The spotting of patterns is a difficult skill to teach but some of the more common sequences such as square or triangle numbers occur often so the pupil should become more familiar with these sequences with experience. By summarising findings clearly the spotting of patterns is made much easier. Several problems have a symmetry about their answers and this often proves to be important when finding a solution.

5 Generalising the results

Pupils are often asked to find relationships or to construct formulas. This is different from simply spotting a pattern which can be used to generate further terms. For example, the 20th term of a triangle number sequence can be found by adding all the whole numbers 1 to 20 or by extending a table of results. The generalisation which gives the number is $20 \times 21 \div 2$, or the nth term is $n(n + 1) \div 2$. A generalisation may not use algebra – it may be a written statement such as: 'Take the number and add 1 to it. Multiply the new number by the original number and divide the answer by 2.'

6 Testing the generalisation

This is often omitted by pupils. They have a tendency to generalise too early in a problem and therefore base their generalisation on insufficient examples or make a guess from examples which are not all correct. To test a generalisation or formula, pupils must assume that their statement is true and should then use it to predict an unknown quantity. This should then be verified in the problem by using a different method; for example, by extending a number pattern or by drawing a suitable diagram.

7 Explain the generalisation carefully

This does not require a complete mathematical proof (although capable pupils should not be discouraged from attempting this!); rather, it gives an insight to the pupil's thinking. It is helpful in assessing their full knowledge of the problem. It is also important for pupils to explain mathematical processes carefully.

Example The sum of the first n odd numbers is n^2, and is explained by this diagram.

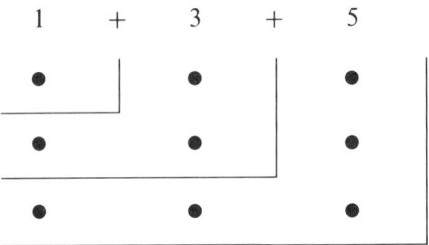

8 Explaining any weakness in the generalisation

Often when pupils reach the point of generalising their results they stop. However, in many problems a simple formula will not work for all situations. Either there are special cases in the problem or the full solution is in more than one part. (There may be one formula for the odd case and another for the even case.) The pupils should be encouraged to show when their generalisation falls down and to try to explain why. These pitfalls will probably be revealed when pupils test their generalisation.

9 Extra work beyond that asked in the question

For open investigations pupils should be encouraged to look beyond the question. The very nature of investigational work is open, so that if a pupil finds a connection or relationship or even a relevant fact that has not been specifically asked for it should be reflected in the mark given to the work. On the other hand, when the pupils have worked through a structured investigation they may be able to extend it themselves.

Assessing a structured investigation

The structured investigations are written in a way which is designed to help pupils learn how to tackle a problem. The answers given in the solution have a one-to-one correspondence with the questions, but are not examples of ideal solutions. Pupils may have different but equally valid answers, and consideration should be given to these differences when assessing the work. It must also be noted that the structured questions give the pupils basic examples to tackle, ask them to summarise the results and to find patterns. Clearly these three skills cannot be fully assessed by using the structured questions. With the structured investigation the teacher may wish, and is probably best advised, to give a simple grade rather than an elaborate assessment.

Here is an example of a solution to the structured version of 'Petfood pile' produced by a 14 year old pupil in the top percentile range.

Petfood pile

Sheldon, a shelf filler at Fine Flair supermarket, has been asked to display Kattosnacks, a new brand of cat food. He has been told to stack the tins against a window and that each tin must be supported by two tins underneath it. This means that the shape of the complete display is always a triangle.

If he builds a pile two tins wide on the bottom row he has a total of three tins in the pile, like this.

1 How many tins would there be in a pile that has three tins on the bottom row? This is called a 3 wide triangular pile.
2 Draw a 4 wide triangular pile.
3 How many tins are there in a 4 wide triangular pile?
4 Copy and complete this table.

Width of triangular pile	1	2	3	4	5	6
Number of tins in pile		3				

5 How many tins are there in a 10 wide triangular pile?
6 How many extra tins are needed to change a 10 wide triangular pile into an 11 wide triangular pile?
7 How many extra tins are needed to change a 17 wide triangular pile into an 18 wide triangular pile?

New York Cop and other investigations © Cambridge University Press 1988

Petfood file

Sheldon is told to stack two different flavours of Kattosnacks (chicken and beef) together in the same pile for a window display. To save work he changes the shape of the triangular pile of Kattosnacks

from 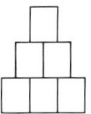 to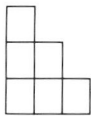

The number of tins is the same – only the shape has been altered. He adds the same number of beef Kattosnacks tins on top of the chicken Kattosnacks pile like this.

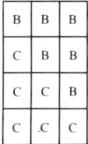

The beef Kattosnacks makes a triangle the same size but the other way up. This is now a rectangular pile.

8 Draw a 4 wide rectangular pile made up of two 4 wide triangular piles.
9 When Sheldon joins two 4 wide triangular piles together, how high is the rectangular pile?
10 Copy and complete this table.

Width of rectangular pile	1	2	3	4	5
Height of rectangular pile	2		4		

11 What is the connection between the width of a rectangular pile and its height?
12 In any rectangular pile, what can you say about the number of chicken Kattosnacks and the number of beef Kattosnacks tins?
13 How many tins are there in a rectangular pile that is 3 tins wide?
14 Copy and complete this table.

Width of rectangular pile	1	2	3	4	5
Number of tins in pile	2				

15 How many tins are there in a rectangular pile 20 tins wide? How many are beef flavour and how many are chicken flavour?
16 How many tins would there be in a rectangular pile that is *n* tins wide?
17 How many tins of chicken Kattosnacks are there in a rectangular pile 30 tins wide?
18 How many tins of chicken Kattosnacks are there in a rectangular pile *n* tins wide?

New York Cop and other investigations © Cambridge University Press 1988

APY 3A1   Petfood Pile

1.) If Sheldon builds a pile that has 3 tins on the bottom row he would have a pile that looked like this:-

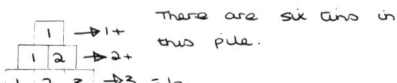

There are six tins in this pile.

2.) If he builds a pile that has 4 tins on the bottom row he would have a pile that looked like this:-

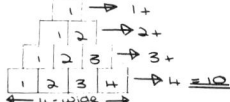

3.) As you can see there are 10 tins in a 4-wide triangular pile.

4.) This is a 5-wide triangular pile:-

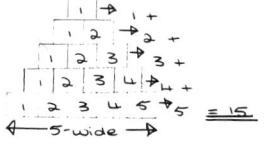

And, this is a 6-wide triangular pile.

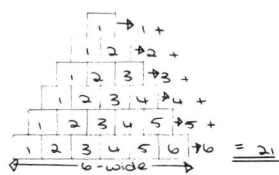

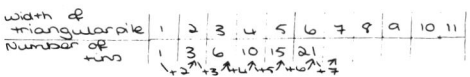

5.) You can probably pick out the pattern in this table. According to this table the number of tins on a 7-wide triangular pile should be 21 + 7 = 28.

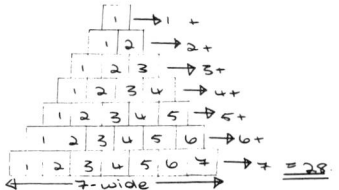

This pile prooves that the pattern is correct so the rest of the table can now be filled in.

③

This table shows that there are 55 tins needed in a 10-wide triangular pile.

6.) To make a 10-wide pile into an 11-wide pile all you do is add the bottom row of tins, 11.

Here are some examples of this.

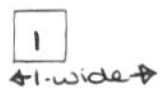

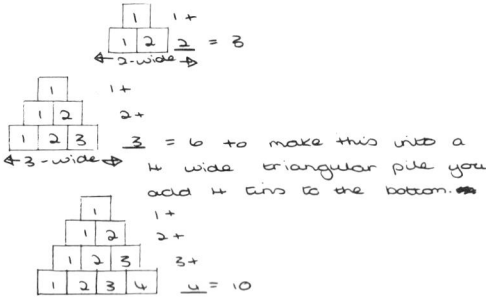

to make this into a 2-wide triangular pile you add the bottom row of tins

= 6 to make this into a 4 wide triangular pile you add 4 tins to the bottom.

= 10

7.) To change a 17-wide pile into an 18-wide pile you would need 18 tins to add to the bottom row.

8.) Now the shape for stacking tins has been altered from a triangular pile to a rectangular. So a four-wide pile of tins consisting of two 4-wide triangular piles looked like this:-

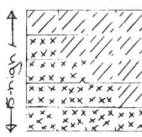

= Beef

= Chicken

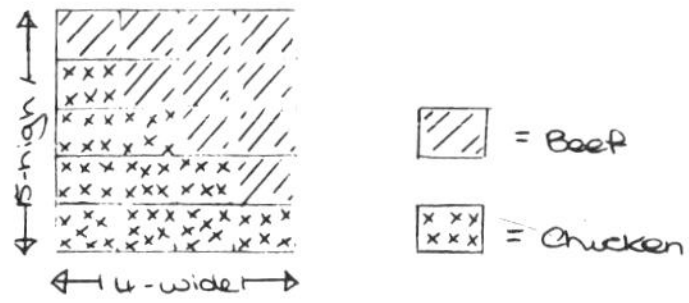

9.) When the two 4-wide triangular piles are added together as above the rectangle is 5 tins high.

(a) 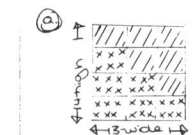 Here are some more examples of rectangular piles.

(c)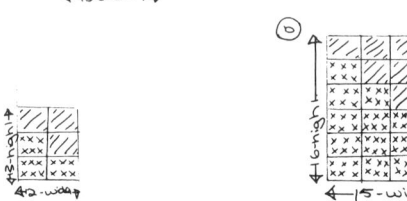

(b)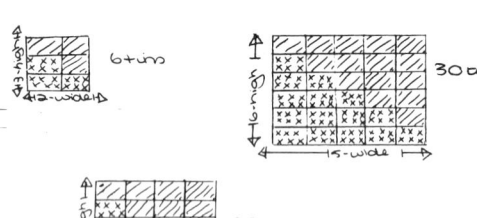

⑤

10.)

Number of tins in the bottom row of pile	Number of tins up the side of the pile
1	2
2	3
3	4
4	5
5	6
6	7
7	8
8	9
9	10
10	11

11.) The connection between the width and height of a rectangular pile is the width of the pile plus one is the height. This can be written as:-

$$W + 1 = H.$$

(W = width H = height.)

12.) In any rectangular pile done in this way you can always say that the number of beef tins and the number of chicken tins is always the same.

13.) In a rectangular pile 3 tins wide there are 12 tins altogether.

14.)

Width of rectangular pile	Number of tins in a rectangular pile
1	2
2	6
3	12
4	20
5	30

P.T.O. for examples

6 tins

30 tins

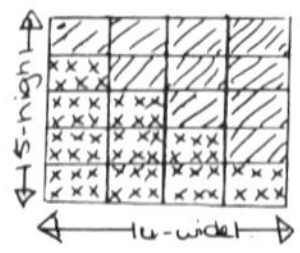

20 tins

15.) There are 420 tins in a 20-wide rectangular pile.

16.) There would be $(n+1)n$ tins in a rectangular pile n tins wide.

17.) There are 930 tins in a pile 30 tins wide, therefore there are 465 chicken tins in a rectangular pile 30 tins wide.

18.) There are $\frac{(n+1)n}{2}$ tins in a pile n tins wide. Because the height is always the width plus 1 (ie $n+1$) multiplied by the width (ie $(n+1)n$ will give you the area or the number of tins altogether. To then find the number of chicken tins you simply divide by 2 (ie $\frac{(n+1)n}{2}$)

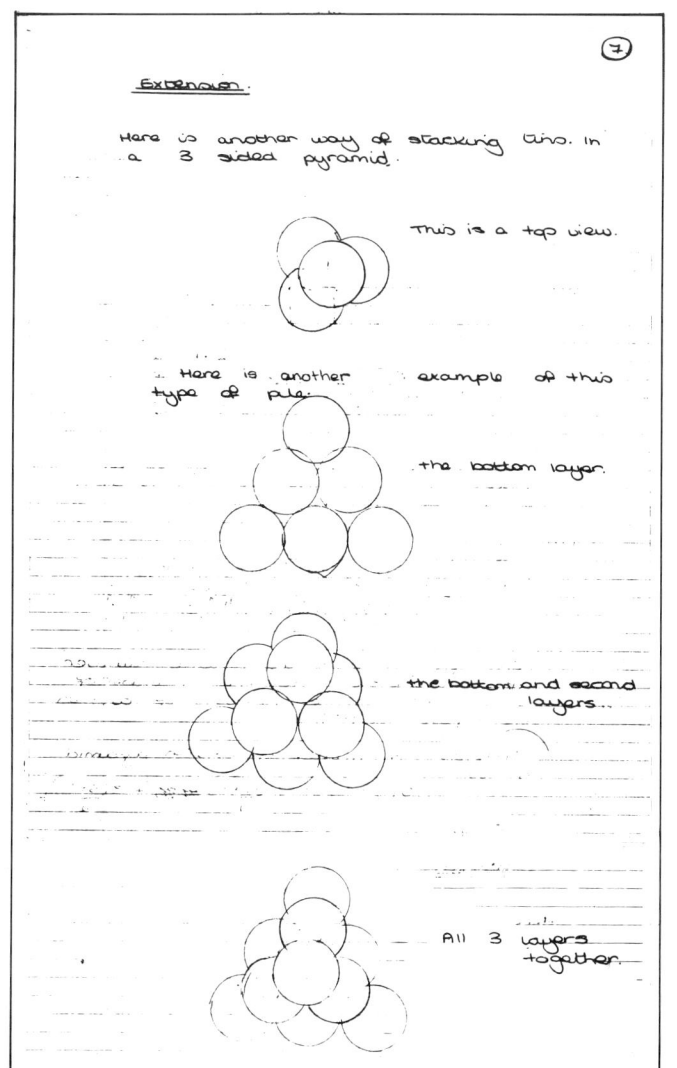
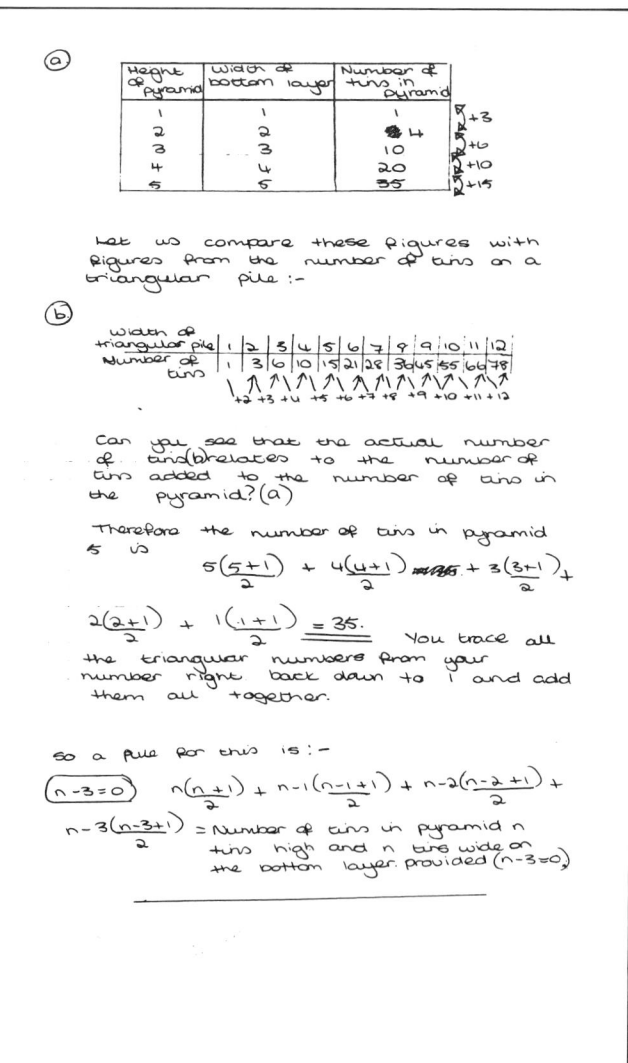

From this solution it is possible to see the high quality of work that can be produced. The main points of note are:

1. The depth to which the investigation can be taken. In an open investigation it would be much more difficult to find the relationship $n(n+1) \div 2$ without the aid of the structure of the question.

2. Pupils are used to looking at a set of numbers to find a relationship. However, in this investigation the process of finding a generalisation is much more complicated. First, the pupil must identify a spatial pattern, then transpose this pattern into a numerical equivalent and then use the initial spatial understanding to generalise the numerical information. The structured format has helped the pupil with this process. The ability to visualise patterns makes the generalisation much easier to formulate and to use.

3. The more able pupil can extend the question using their own ideas and can produce interesting and valuable work without the aid of a structured framework. The two most popular extensions for this piece of work were found to be 'tetrahedron stacking' as has been attempted by this pupil, and 'square-based pyramid stacking'. Other unusual methods of stacking have been suggested (some of which would have been impractical) but these still allowed the pupils to generate further work and relationships.

4. The structured question offers a sound basis for pupils to develop their report writing skills.

Assessing an open investigation

The open investigations give the teacher the best opportunity to assess the pupils' ability to solve problems. It is better to assess this type of investigation using a detailed marking scheme, an example of which is set out below.

Marking scheme for 'Petfood pile'

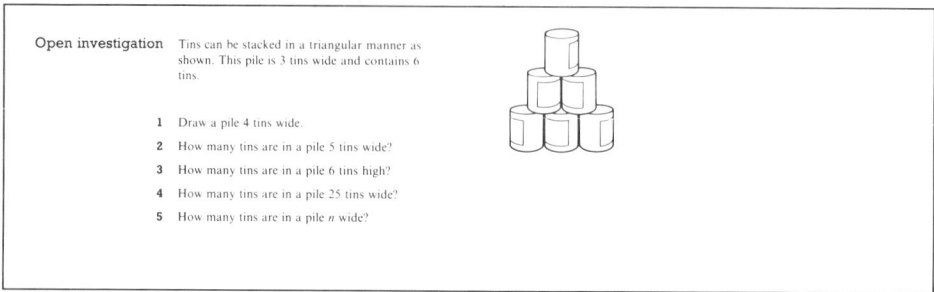

Open investigation Tins can be stacked in a triangular manner as shown. This pile is 3 tins wide and contains 6 tins.

1 Draw a pile 4 tins wide.
2 How many tins are in a pile 5 tins wide?
3 How many tins are in a pile 6 tins high?
4 How many tins are in a pile 25 tins wide?
5 How many tins are in a pile n wide?

		Mark	
1	Drawing the correct arrangement.	1	
2	Working out the correct number of tins.	1	
3	Working out the correct number of tins.	1	
4	Correct result. (325)	4	
	A systematic approach to the solution but the answer is wrong.		2
5	Correct statement of the relationship either in an algebraic form or by a clear statement.	7	
	(a) A statement of the result that lacks clarity.		4
	(b) A qualitative description of the relationship; e.g. 'Each time you add an extra row you add one more than the existing height of the pile so you add all the numbers 1, 2, 3, ... up to n.'		3
	(c) A quantitative description of the relationship; e.g. an organised, tabulated set of results.		2

Extra marks: 1 mark for each point noted that has merit; e.g. a clear explanation of how the rule works, or testing a formula produced to see if it works correctly. Up to 3

Total possible mark 17

The marks for questions 1, 2 and 3 are straightforward. Correct answers to these questions show that a pupil has a basic understanding of the situation presented and is able to answer simple questions containing easily manageable numbers.

A correct answer to question 4 shows that a pupil is able to recognise patterns in the numbers produced and can extend that pattern to a situation which is difficult to display diagramatically. It may be that the pupil sees the pattern but calculates the answer incorrectly. If it is clear that a systematic approach has been used that would generate the correct answer then two marks should be awarded.

A correct answer to question 5 shows that a pupil has the ability to generalise the results. The two most common answers for this question are $n(n + 1) \div 2$ and $(n^2 + n) \div 2$. Other ways of writing the relationship should not be ruled out: for example, a statement like 'Multiply the width of the pile by one more than the width and then halve the answer'. Seven marks should be awarded for these or similar answers. The subgroups of marks allow for different levels of sophistication in the pupils' answers.

(a) A statement of results that lacks clarity may be too long winded which makes it difficult to understand. There may be a particular misuse of language: 'times by 2' instead of 'times by itself' without any worked example to clarify the meaning.

(b) A qualitative description may be of the form 'Add all the numbers 1, 2, 3, 4 up to

12

n' or 'Each time you add an extra row you add one more than the existing height of the pile. You can do this until you add *n* on.'

(c) A quantitive description may be an organised table of results showing how the numbers are generated.

Marks should be awarded for answers to question 5 no matter where they appear on the script.

The extra marks should be awarded for ideas which show a particular insight into the relationship. 'If two triangular piles of the same height are put together then a rectangular pile can be made of height *n* + 1 and width *n*. The number of tins in the rectangular pile is *n* (*n* + 1) so in each triangular pile there will be *n* (*n* + 1) ÷ 2.' Again this may come within the solutions to questions 4 and 5 and they need not be written in a formal way. A pupil may apply the formula they have found to check that it works for all situations or write that it will only work for piles made in two dimensions. All ideas of this kind can be awarded one mark each up to a maximum of three marks. These should show a particular insight into the question.

Here are five examples of pieces of work produced by 13 year old pupils. They have been assessed using the above marking scheme and show the various levels of understanding.

Example 1 This pupil has been able to draw the basic examples but is unable to transfer the idea into numerical terms. A lack of understanding of the situation is obvious. Mark achieved: 2.

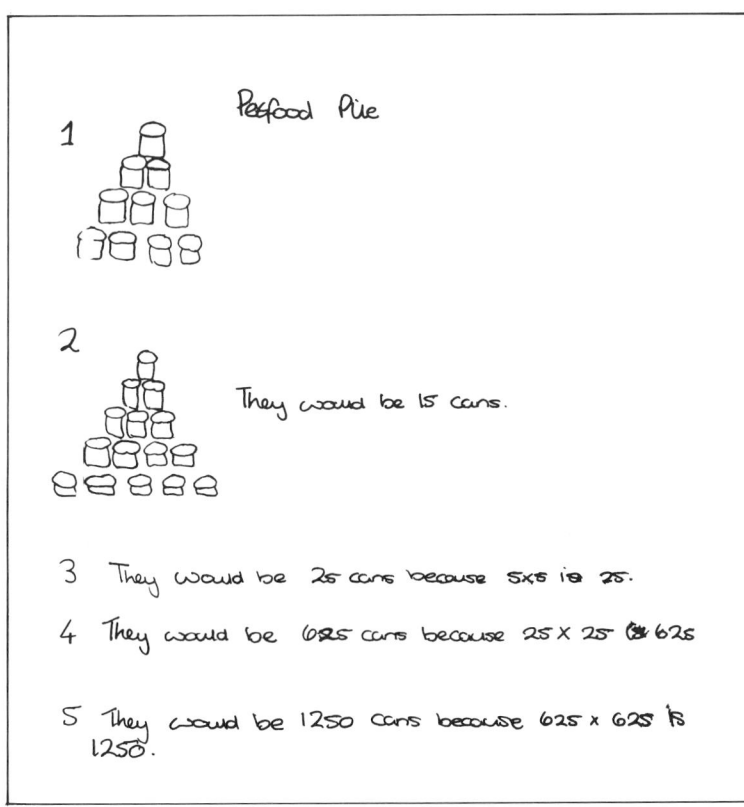

Example 2 A straightforward answer with no working shown. This is very weak in explanation but the pupil has an understanding of the situation because he was able to generate the answer to question 4. Mark achieved: 7.

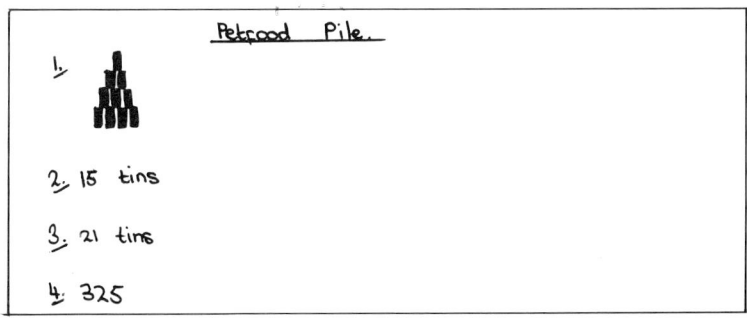

Example 3 Similar to 2 but he has given an indication of how the table can be extended. Mark achieved: 9.

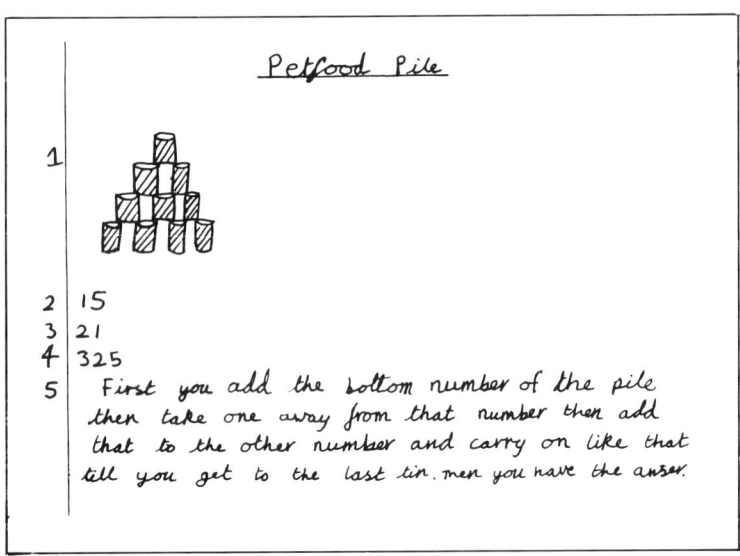

Example 4 This gives an accurate description of how any number in the sequence can be generated. Mark achieved: 10.

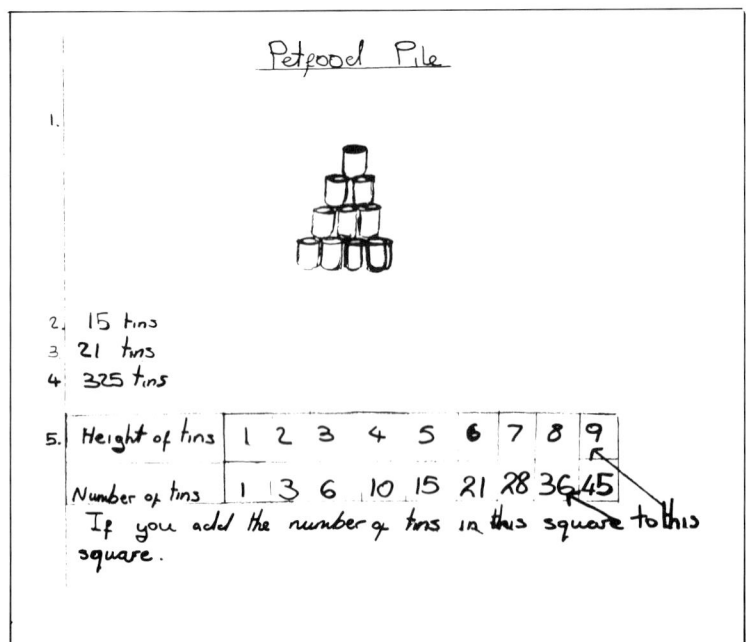

Example 5 A complete investigation with a good clear generalisation found. The extra mark has been awarded because she has checked the generalisation with known results. Mark achieved: 15.

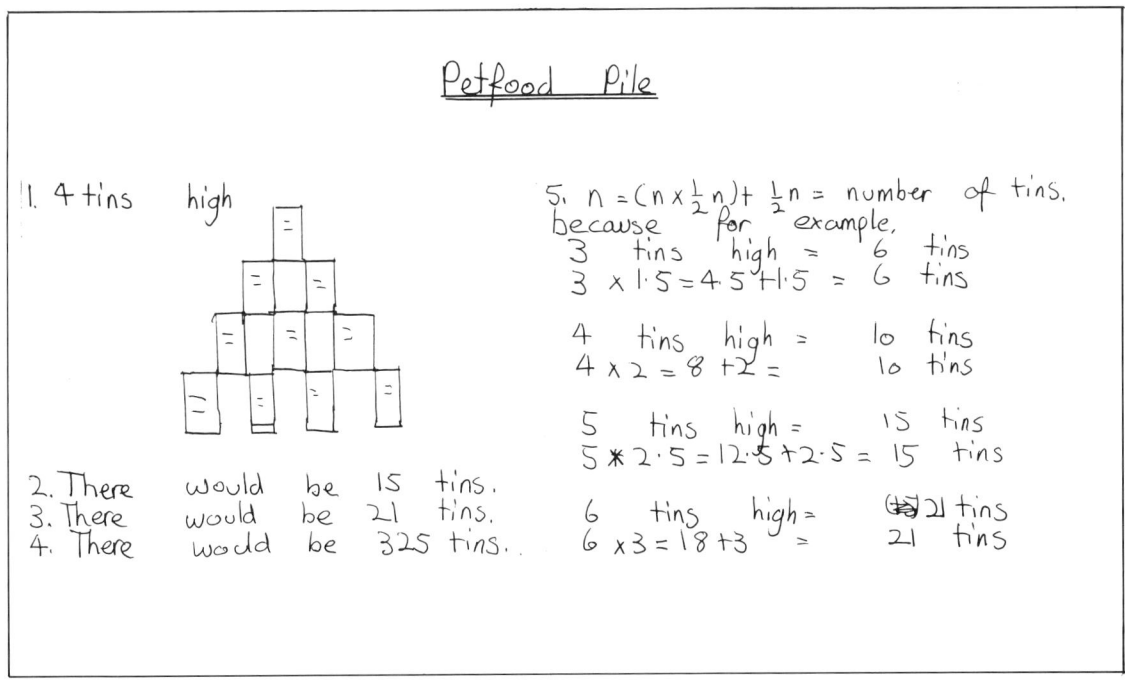

These examples have been included to help teachers with their assessment. It is impossible to list the multitude of ideas produced by pupils, so that a degree of judgement must be exercised by the person marking the work. No two markers will agree on every point but a high degree of concensus will develop with experience. Similar marking schemes can be devised for all open investigations.

Flow chart

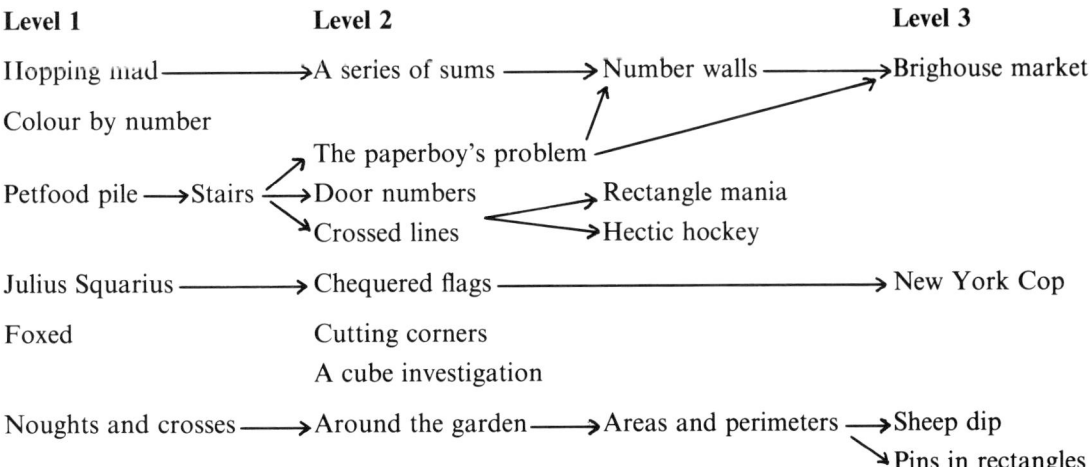

This flow chart is simply a guide to show a sensible route through the investigations in this book. The investigations in level 1 form a foundation for those in higher levels, but are not a prerequisite. The arrows are drawn to show where a concept is consolidated at a higher level.

Not all pupils will be able to successfully attempt the investigations in level 3 so it is important to make reference to the range of ability table in the notes accompanying each investigation.

Hopping mad

Friskie Frog wishes to cross a river. She does not like getting her feet wet so she is going to use stepping stones.

She can jump two gaps with a long hop.

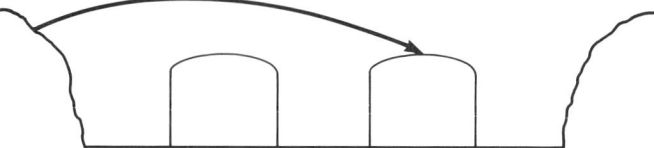

With a short hop she can only jump one gap.

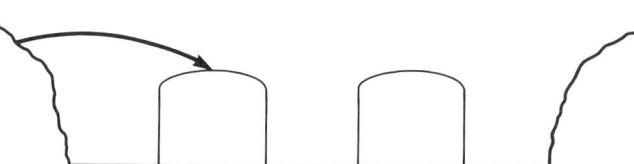

To cross where there are two stepping stones she can either do three short hops, which can be written down (s, s, s) ...

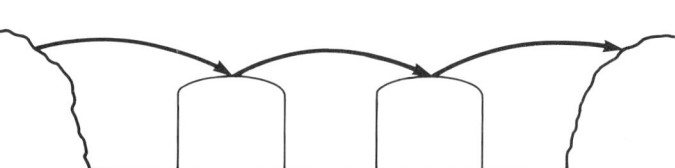

... or she can make a long hop followed by a short hop, which can be written down (l, s).

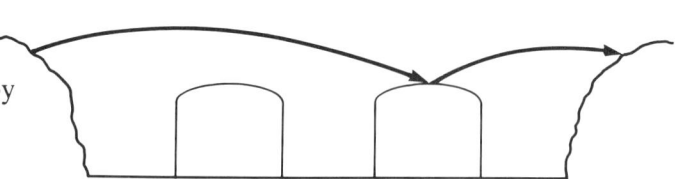

1 There is another way for her to cross the river at a point where there are two stepping stones. Write it down.

On her way home she sees another crossing place where there are three stepping stones.

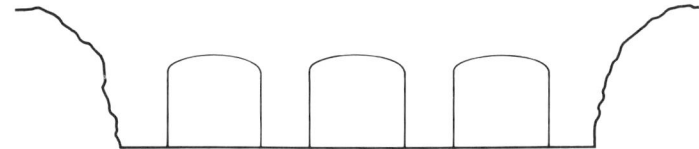

2 How many different ways can she cross the river at this point? List all the ways.

3 Now try to find how many different ways there are of crossing the river for different numbers of stepping stones. Record your results in a table.

Number of stepping stones	0	1	2	3	4	...
Number of different ways of crossing	1					

4 Find a rule that links each of the numbers in the bottom row of the table.

5 How many different ways will there be to cross the river at a point where there are nine stepping stones?

6 Find out the name of this sequence of numbers.

New York Cop and other investigations

Hopping mad

Notes

Objectives · To develop the ability to recognise and generate the Fibonacci series.

Open investigation The opening paragraphs of the investigation without any description of a notation system followed by 'If there were more stepping stones, would there be a pattern in the number of ways to cross the river? Investigate.'

Range of ability

	Ability	100–	80–	60–40
Age	13	6	6	6
	14	Ext	6	6
	15/16	/	/	/

Pre-knowledge Little more than addition of whole numbers and systematic organisation.

Equipment Usual classroom equipment.

Extensions If the frog extends her range of jumps so that she can jump one gap (s), two gaps (m) and three gaps (l), a different sequence of numbers is generated for different numbers of stepping stones.

Solutions

1 The other way to cross the river using two stepping stones is (s, l).

2 There are five ways with three stepping stones.
   (s, s, s, s, s)
   (l, s, s)
   (s, l, s)
   (s, s, l)
   (l, l)

3
Number of stepping stones	0	1	2	3	4	5	6	7	8	9
Number of different ways of crossing	1	2	3	5	8	13	21	34	55	89

4 The nth number in the sequence is the sum of the $(n-1)$th and the $(n-2)$th.
   $$u_n = u_{n-1} + u_{n-2}$$

5 There are 89 different ways of crossing the river where there are nine stepping stones.

6 The sequence is called the Fibonacci sequence.

Colour by number

Pat Painter receives a painting by numbers set from Willie Smudge. The picture must be painted with three different colours (red, yellow and purple).

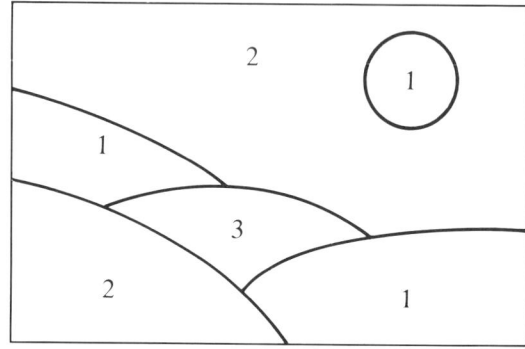

Pat isn't sure which colour to use first. She thinks about painting all the red parts first, then all the yellow parts and finally all the purple parts. This can be written as (R, Y, P). She then thinks about another way of painting the picture. She still paints all the red parts first, but then all the purple parts second and finally all the yellow parts. This she then writes down as (R, P, Y).

1 List all the different ways in which she could have painted the picture if she had decided to use the yellow paint first. Use the above notation.

2 If she had decided to use the purple paint first, list all the different ways of painting the picture.

3 What is the total number of different ways of painting the picture?

4 Willie's next painting set is special because it only has two colours, black (B) and gold (G). List the different ways in which Pat can paint it.

5 Another painting by numbers set has four colours: red, yellow, blue and green. In how many different ways can this picture be painted starting with the red paint? List all the different ways using the letters R, Y, B and G.

6 Find the number of different ways of painting the picture starting with the yellow paint.

7 How many different ways are there of painting the picture starting with the blue paint?

8 Write down the number of ways of painting the picture using the green paint first. You do not have to list them.

9 What is the total number of different ways of painting the four colour picture?

10 Copy and complete this table.

Number of colours	1	2	3	4	5	6
Number of different ways of painting the picture	1					

11 How many different ways could a picture be painted if there were 11 different colours?

12 Write down a rule to give the number of different ways of colouring a picture if you are given the number of colours to use.

New York Cop and other investigations 18 © Cambridge University Press 1988

Colour by number

Notes

Objectives
- To develop the ability to list in an orderly and systematic way.
- To introduce the concept of factorials.

Open investigation Use the introduction as given in the structured investigation followed by:

1. List all the different ways in which she could have painted a picture using three different colours.
2. In how many different ways could she paint a picture with four colours?
3. Investigate the number of ways she could paint a picture with different numbers of colours.

Range of ability

Age	Ability	100–	80–	60–40
	13	12	11	11
	14	Ext	12	11
	15/16	/	/	12

Pre-knowledge This is a basic investigation so little knowledge is assumed beyond an ability to use arithmetic.

Equipment Normal classroom equipment.

Extensions In how many different ways can n people sit on a row of n chairs?

How many different arrangements of n people around a circular table with n chairs are there? Only the order not the position is important.

Solutions

1. (Y, P, R) (Y, R, P)
2. (P, Y, R) (P, R, Y)
3. 6
4. (B, G) (G, B)
5. (R, Y, B, G) (R, G, B, Y) (R, B, G, Y)
   (R, Y, G, B) (R, G, Y, B) (R, B, Y, G)
6. 6 different ways
7. 6
8. 6
9. 24
10.

Number of colours	1	2	3	4	5	6
Number of different ways of painting the picture	1	2	6	24	120	720

11. 39 916 800
12. With n different colours there will be $n(n-1)(n-2)\ldots 3 \times 2 \times 1 = n!$ different ways of painting the picture, i.e. $n!$ ways.

Petfood pile

Sheldon, a shelf filler at Fine Flair supermarket, has been asked to display Kattosnacks, a new brand of cat food. He has been told to stack the tins against a window and that each tin must be supported by two tins underneath it. This means that the shape of the complete display is always a triangle.

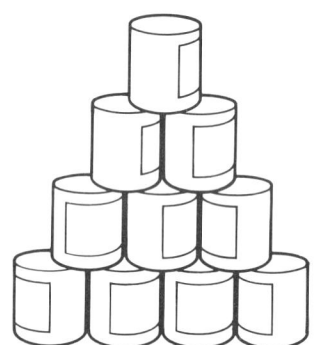

If he builds a pile two tins wide on the bottom row he has a total of three tins in the pile, like this.

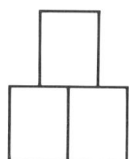

1. How many tins would there be in a pile that has three tins on the bottom row? This is called a 3 wide triangular pile.

2. Draw a 4 wide triangular pile.

3. How many tins are there in a 4 wide triangular pile?

4. Copy and complete this table.

Width of triangular pile	1	2	3	4	5	6
Number of tins in pile		3				

5. How many tins are there in a 10 wide triangular pile?

6. How many extra tins are needed to change a 10 wide triangular pile into an 11 wide triangular pile?

7. How many extra tins are needed to change a 17 wide triangular pile into an 18 wide triangular pile?

New York Cop and other investigations © Cambridge University Press 1988

Petfood file

Sheldon is told to stack two different flavours of Kattosnacks (chicken and beef) together in the same pile for a window display. To save work he changes the shape of the triangular pile of Kattosnacks

from 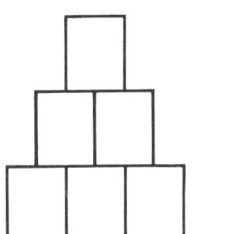 to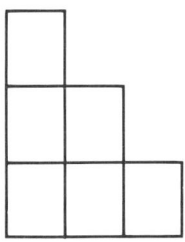

The number of tins is the same – only the shape has been altered. He adds the same number of beef Kattosnacks tins on top of the chicken Kattosnacks pile like this.

B	B	B
C	B	B
C	C	B
C	C	C

The beef Kattosnacks makes a triangle the same size but the other way up. This is now a rectangular pile.

8   Draw a 4 wide rectangular pile made up of two 4 wide triangular piles.

9   When Sheldon joins two 4 wide triangular piles together, how high is the rectangular pile?

10 Copy and complete this table.

Width of rectangular pile	1	2	3	4	5
Height of rectangular pile	2		4		

11 What is the connection between the width of a rectangular pile and its height?

12 In any rectangular pile, what can you say about the number of chicken Kattosnacks and the number of beef Kattosnacks tins?

13 How many tins are there in a rectangular pile that is 3 tins wide?

14 Copy and complete this table.

Width of rectangular pile	1	2	3	4	5
Number of tins in pile	2				

15 How many tins are there in a rectangular pile 20 tins wide? How many are beef flavour and how many are chicken flavour?

16 How many tins would there be in a rectangular pile that is n tins wide?

17 How many tins of chicken Kattosnacks are there in a rectangular pile 30 tins wide?

18 How many tins of chicken Kattosnacks are there in a rectangular pile n tins wide?

New York Cop and other investigations   **21**   © Cambridge University Press 1988

Petfood pile

Notes

Objectives
- To familiarise pupils with the sequence of triangle numbers.
- To recognise and generate the sequence of triangle numbers.
- To construct a formula to calculate the nth term of the sequence of triangle numbers.

Open investigation Tins can be stacked in a triangular manner as shown. This pile is 3 tins wide and contains 6 tins.

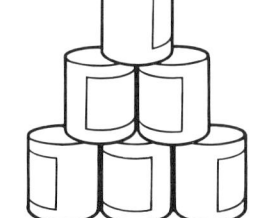

1. Draw a pile 4 tins wide.
2. How many tins are in a pile 5 tins wide?
3. How many tins are in a pile 6 tins high?
4. How many tins are in a pile 25 tins wide?
5. How many tins are in a pile n wide?

Range of ability

	Ability	100–	80–	60–40
Age	13	18	7	5
	14	18	15	7
	15/16	Ext	18	15

Pre-knowledge
- Use of letters to represent numbers.
- Simple intuitive algebraic manipulation.

Equipment Tins or cubes or similar objects that can be stacked.

Extensions Exploration of different methods of stacking the tins. For example, tetrahedral or pyramidal stacks will generate different sequences.

Solutions

1. 6

2.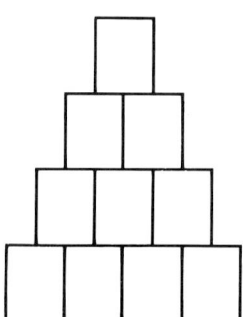

3. 10

4.
Width of triangular pile	1	2	3	4	5	6
Number of tins in pile	1	3	6	10	15	21

5 55

6 11

7 18

8

B	B	B	B
C	B	B	B
C	C	B	B
C	C	C	B
C	C	C	C

9 5

10

Width of rectangular pile	1	2	3	4	5
Height of rectangular pile	2	3	4	5	6

11 The height is one more than the width.

12 They will be the same.

13 12

14

Width of rectangular pile	1	2	3	4	5
Number of tins in pile	2	6	12	20	30

15 420 tins, 210 of each kind.

16 $n(n + 1)$

17 465

18 $\dfrac{n(n + 1)}{2}$

Stairs

This is an 'up and down' staircase. It is 4 steps high and is made from 16 cubes.

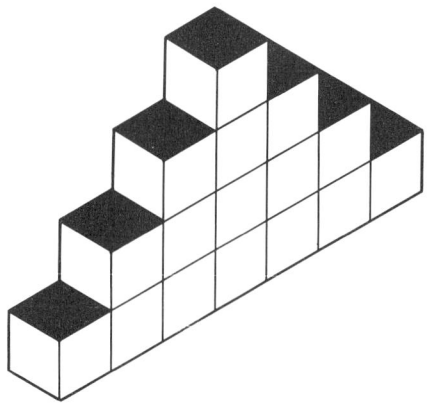

1. Draw a 3 high 'up and down' staircase.
2. How many cubes are needed to make a 3 high 'up and down' staircase?
3. How many cubes are needed to make a 2 high 'up and down' staircase?
4. Copy and complete this table.

Height of 'up and down' staircase	1	2	3	4	5	6	7
Number of cubes used				16			

5. How many cubes would be required to make a 20 high 'up and down' staircase?
6. What is the name of the sequence of numbers in the 'Number of cubes' row of the table?
7. How many cubes would be required to make an n high 'up and down' staircase?

This is an 'up' staircase. It is 4 steps high and is made from 10 cubes.

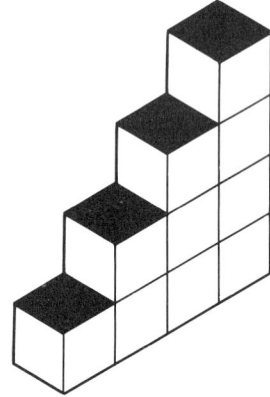

8. Draw an 'up' staircase 3 steps high.
9. How many cubes would be required to make a 3 high 'up' staircase?
10. How many cubes would be required to make a 5 high 'up' staircase?
11. Copy and complete this table.

Height of 'up' staircase	1	2	3	4	5	6	7
Number of cubes used				10			

12. How many cubes are needed to make a 20 high 'up' staircase?

New York Cop and other investigations

Stairs

This is a 4 high 'up and down' staircase.

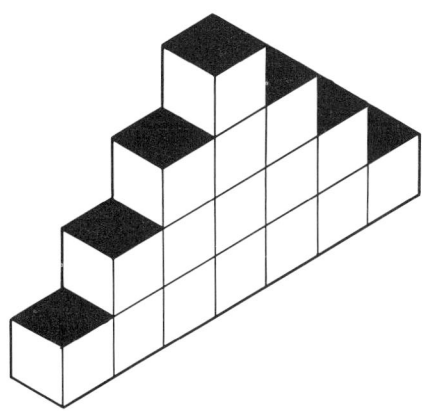

This is a staircase made from two 4 high 'up' staircases put together. It is called a 4 high 'double up' staircase.

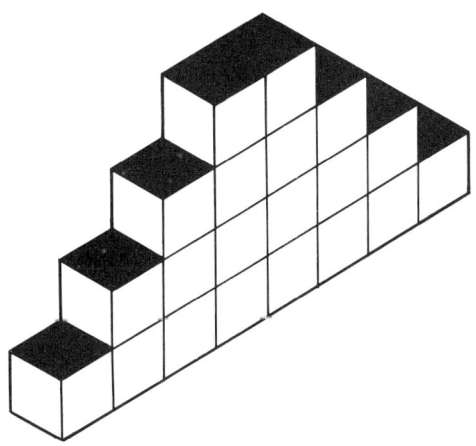

13 How many more cubes are required to make a 4 high 'double up' staircase from a 4 high 'up and down' staircase?

14 How many cubes are needed altogether to make a 4 high 'double up' staircase?

15 Draw a 3 high 'double up' staircase.

16 How many more cubes are required to make a 3 high 'double up' staircase from a 3 high 'up and down' staircase?

17 How many cubes are needed altogether to make a 3 high 'double up' staircase?

18 How many cubes would be needed to make a 20 high 'double up' staircase?

19 How many cubes would be needed to make an n high 'double up' staircase?

20 How many cubes would be needed to make an n high 'up' staircase?

Stairs

Notes

Objectives
- To familiarise pupils with the square and triangle number sequences.
- To help pupils recognise square numbers away from situations involving squares themselves.
- To construct formulas for the nth term of the square and triangle number sequences.
- To help pupils recognise the link between square and triangle numbers.

Open investigation Use the introduction as given in the structured investigation up to question 2 followed by:

3 Investigate the number of cubes needed to make other sizes of 'up and down' staircases.

This 'up' staircase is 4 steps high and is made from 10 cubes.

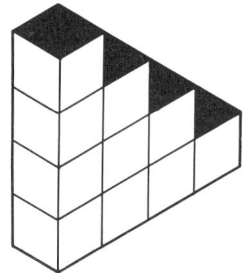

4 How many cubes would be needed to make a 5 high 'up' staircase?

5 Investigate the number of cubes needed to make other sizes of 'up' staircases.

6 What is the relationship between an n high 'up and down' staircase and an n high 'up' staircase?

Range of ability

Ability	100–	80–	60–40
Age 13	20	12	12
14	Ext	20	12
15/16	Ext	Ext	20

Pre-knowledge
- Use of letters to represent numbers.
- Simple intuitive algebraic manipulation.

Equipment Cubes are useful for making the staircases. Isometric or triangular spotty paper can be used in drawing the staircases. (A master for triangular spotty paper is included at the back of this book.)

Extensions These staircases have depth equal to their height. How many cubes would be needed to make an n high staircase?

 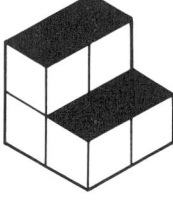 

Solutions

1

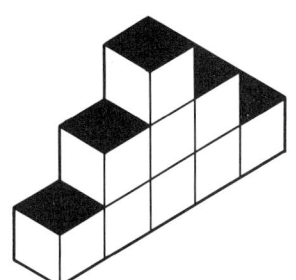

2 9

3 4

4

Height of 'up and down' staircase	1	2	3	4	5	6	7
Number of cubes used	1	4	9	16	25	36	49

5 400

6 Square numbers

7 n^2

8

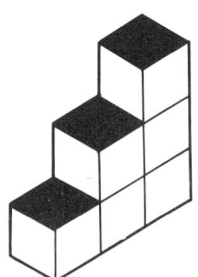

9 6

10 15

11

Height of 'up' staircase	1	2	3	4	5	6	7
Number of cubes used	1	3	6	10	15	21	28

12 210

13 4

14 20

15

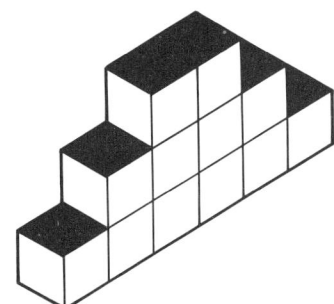

16 3

17 12

18 420

19 $n^2 + n$

20 $(n^2 + n) \div 2$

Julius Squarius

Julius Squarius, a Roman Centurion, was very keen on tiling his square rooms and courtyards with square tiles. One day he was watching his tiler laying a new floor.

This was the 3 by 3 square which the tiler had already laid.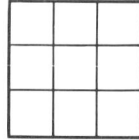

1 How many tiles had the tiler laid?

The tiler then laid some more tiles so that he reached the next possible square shape (a 4 by 4 square).

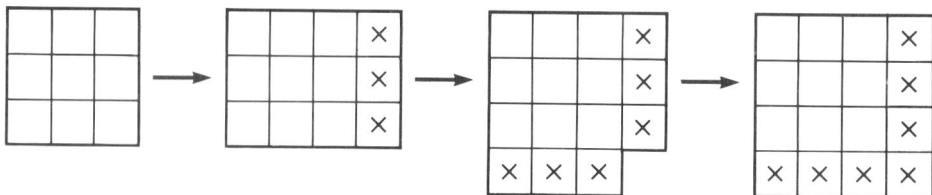

2 How many tiles were added to the 3 by 3 square to get the 4 by 4 square?

3 How many tiles in total were used to make the 4 by 4 square?

4 Show the four stages which the tiler would use to go from a 4 by 4 square to a 5 by 5 square.

5 How many extra tiles would be added to go from the 4 by 4 to the 5 by 5 square?

6 How many tiles would be used in total to make the 5 by 5 square?

The tiler then worked to make a 6 by 6 square.

7 How many extra tiles would he need?

8 How many tiles would be used in total to make the 6 by 6 square?

9 Copy and complete this table.

Size of square	1 by 1	2 by 2	3 by 3	...	7 by 7
Number of tiles			9		

10 How many tiles would be needed to make a 25 by 25 square?

11 Explain clearly how you reached your last answer.

12 How many tiles would be needed to make a n by n square?

13 How many tiles will be added going from a 24 by 24 square to a 25 by 25 square?

14 Explain clearly how you reached your last answer.

15 How many tiles would be added going from a n by n square to a $(n + 1)$ by $(n + 1)$ square?

New York Cop and other investigations

Julius Squarius

Notes

Objectives
- To introduce pupils to the methods of investigational work.
- To develop the concept of the sequence of square numbers.

Open investigation Use the introduction as given in the structured investigation up to question 3 followed by:

4 Show how the tiler continues his work and find a rule which links the size of the square to the number of tiles used.

Range of ability

Ability	100–	80–	60–40
Age 13	14	14	11
14	Ext	Ext	15
15/16	/	/	/

Pre-knowledge This is a basic investigation so little knowledge is assumed beyond an ability to use arithmetic.

Equipment A large supply of square counters.

Extensions How many squares are there on a chessboard?

Answer: $1^2 + 2^2 + ... + 8^2$

Solutions

1 9

2 7

3 16

4
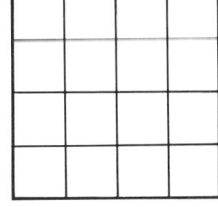 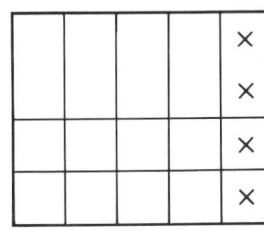

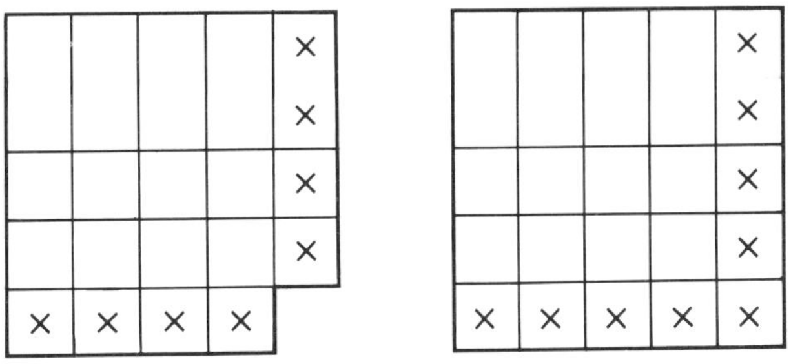

5 9

6 25

7 11

8 36

9
Size of square	1 by 1	2 by 2	3 by 3	4 by 4	5 by 5	6 by 6	7 by 7
Number of tiles	1	4	9	16	25	36	49

10 625

11 25 rows of 25 is equal to 625.

12 n^2

13 49

14 2 lots of 24 plus another 1

15 $2n + 1$

Foxed

Burrow   Dandelion field

Belinda Bunny lived in a burrow inside Warren Wood. Her favourite food was dandelion leaves which grew in the fields nearby. The most luscious leaves grew in the field two hedges away.

One day when she was eating her lunch a fox appeared and she had to make a quick escape back to her burrow. There was only one gap in each hedge through which she could run, so she had only one escape route. She only just managed to escape from the fox. Belinda was a clever rabbit and back in her burrow she thought about how to increase the number of escape routes through the hedges.

In the night she went out and made an extra hole in each of the two hedges. This increased the number of escape routes, one of which is shown below.

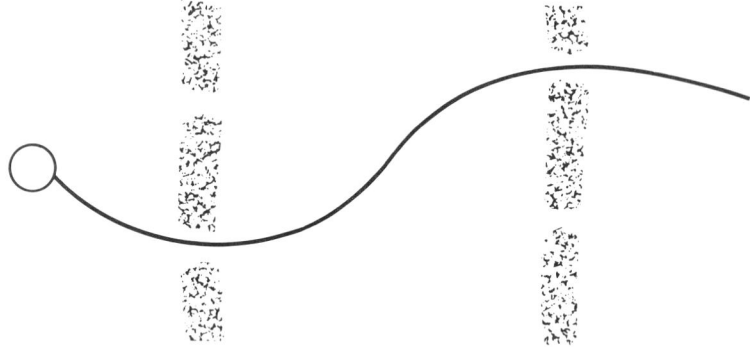

1. With two gaps in each hedge, how many different escape routes from the dandelion field to her burrow were there? (She never went back into a field she had just left.)

After a while she decided that the fox must have learned all her escape routes so she built another gap in one of the hedges.

2. How many different escape routes did she have now?

3. Does it matter in which hedge she made the new gap? Explain your answer.

4. Work out the number of escape routes she had for different numbers of gaps in the two hedges.

5. How many different escape routes would there have been if there were 7 gaps in one hedge and 6 gaps in the other?

6. Explain how you worked out the previous answer.

7. If there had been three hedges to pass through, the first having 2 gaps, the second having 3 gaps and the third having 2 gaps, how many escape routes would there have been?

8. If there had been three hedges to pass through, the first having x gaps, the second having y gaps and the third having z gaps, how many escape routes would there have been?

New York Cop and other investigations © Cambridge University Press 1988

Foxed

Notes

Objectives
- To develop the skill of listing and recording.
- To develop the ability to see a relationship in a situation without there being a number sequence.

Open investigation Use the introduction as given in the structured investigation up to question 3 followed by:

4   Look for a rule that will describe how many routes there are no matter how many hedges or gaps, and try to explain why your rule works.

5   How many routes would there be through ten hedges each with 4 gaps in them?

Range of ability

	Ability	100–	80–	60–40
Age	13	8	7	7
	14	Ext	8	8
	15/16	/	/	/

Pre-knowledge This is a basic investigation so little knowledge is assumed beyond an ability to use arithmetic.

Equipment Normal classroom equipment.

Extensions In an attempt to develop notational skills this investigation can be restated as a listing question rather than a spatial question. For example:

A shop supplies curtains in 3 materials, carpets in 4 colours and wallpaper in 7 designs. In how many different ways can a room be decorated?

Solutions

1   4

2   6

3   It does not matter since 2 holes in the first hedge and 3 holes in the second gives the same number of escape routes as 3 in the first and 2 in the second.

4   The pupil's own results. Check that
The number of   =   number of holes   ×   number of holes
escape routes   in 1st hedge   in 2nd hedge.

5   42

6   Multiply 6 by 7

7   $2 \times 3 \times 2 = 12$

8   Total number of escape routes = $x \times y \times z$

31

A series of sums

Write down two different counting numbers between *Example*
0 and 5, smaller first. 2, 5

Add them together to get a third number and write
this down. $2 + 5 = 7$

Add the second and the third numbers to get a fourth. $5 + 7 = 12$

Add the third and fourth to get a fifth. $7 + 12 = 19$

Finally the fourth and fifth to get a sixth. $12 + 19 = 31$

Sequence: 2, 5, 7, 12, 19, 31

1 Add up all your six numbers and divide by the fifth number in the sequence. What number do you get?

2 Pick two other starting numbers and repeat the procedure above. You may wish to use decimals, or negative numbers.

3 Pick two numbers between 100 and 200 and using a calculator repeat the procedure again.

4 What do you notice about your answers in all three cases?

5 Extend all three sequences until you have ten numbers in each. (Add the fifth to the sixth to get the seventh and so on.)

6 Add up the ten numbers of each sequence and divide each total by the seventh term of each sequence. What do you notice?

Using A as the first number and B as the second number, the sequence becomes
$A, \quad B, \quad A+B, \quad A+2B, \ldots$

7 Copy down this sequence and continue until you have ten terms.

8 Add together the first six
terms of this sequence. $\quad\quad A$
$\quad\quad\quad\quad\quad\quad\quad\quad\quad +\quad\quad\quad B$
How does this total relate $\quad + \quad A \ + \ B$
to the fifth number of $\quad\quad + \quad A \ + \ 2B$
the sequence? $\quad\quad + \quad \ldots$

9 Show that the sum of the first ten numbers is a multiple of the seventh number in the sequence.

10 The relationship between the sum of the first six numbers and the fifth number can be written

Sum (1–6) = $c \times$ 5th   where c is an integer (positive whole number).

What number does c stand for?

11 Sum (1–10) = $d \times$ 7th   What number does d stand for?

12 Write down a statement which links Sum (1–14) and the ninth number in the sequence.

13 Prove this by extending your A and B sequence.

14 Predict what the next sum relationship will be.

15 Try to find other summation statements.

A series of sums

Notes

Objectives
- To develop the skills of algebraic manipulation and proofs using algebra.
- To develop the ability to prove relationships using algebra.

Open investigation Use the introduction as given in the structured investigation up to question 4 followed by:

5 Extend each sequence to ten terms and state a connection between the sum of the ten terms and the seventh term. Prove this using A and B for the first two terms.

6 Extend your letter sequence further and find relationships for the sum of the first 14 terms and the first 18 terms.

7 Try to find other sum relationships.

Range of ability

	Ability	100–	80–	60–40
Age	13	9	6	–
	14	15	9	6
	15/16	Ext	15	15

Pre-knowledge
- Use of letters to represent numbers.
- Use and manipulation of algebraic terms.

Equipment Usual classroom equipment.

Extensions Investigate the sequence of the multipliers. (The term-to-term rule of this new sequence tends to the Golden Ratio + 1.)

Solutions

1, 2, 3, 4 The result is always 4 regardless of the starting numbers.

5, 6 The sum of the first ten numbers is always 11 times the seventh term.

7
$$
\begin{array}{rcl}
A & & \\
& & B \\
A & + & B \\
A & + & 2B \\
2A & + & 3B \\
3A & + & 5B \\
5A & + & 8B \\
8A & + & 13B \\
13A & + & 21B \\
21A & + & 34B \\
\end{array}
$$

8 The sum of the first six terms is $8A + 12B = 4(2A + 3B) = 4 \times$ 5th term.

9 The sum of the first ten terms is $55A + 88B = 11(5A + 8B) = 11 \times$ 7th term.

10 c stands for 4.

11 d stands for 11.

12 Sum (1–14) = $29 \times$ 9th term.

New York Cop and other investigations © Cambridge University Press 1988

13 11th term $= 34A + 55B$
12th term $= 55A + 89B$
13th term $= 89A + 144B$
14th term $= 144A + 233B$

Sum $(1-14) = 377A + 609B$
$= 29(13A + 21B)$
$= 29 \times$ 9th term.

14 Sum $(1-18) = e \times$ 11th term, where $e = 76$.

15 Sum $(1-22) = 199 \times$ 13th
Sum $(1-26) = 521 \times$ 15th
Sum $(1-30) = 1364 \times$ 17th
Sum $(1-34) = 3571 \times$ 19th
Sum $(1-38) = 9349 \times$ 21st
Sum $(1-42) = 24476 \times$ 23rd.

The paperboy's problem

A paperboy has been given a new round by his newsagent. He finds that he has two papers left to deliver to a terrace of five houses but the newsagent has forgotten to write the house numbers on the papers. Both newspapers are copies of *The Moon* so there is no point in delivering them both to the same house. After some thought he decides to deliver one to the second house and the other to the fourth house, as shown in the diagram.

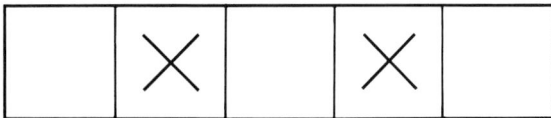

1 How many different ways are there of delivering these two papers to the five houses? Try to set out the different possibilities in an organised way.

On returning to the shop the paperboy explains his problem and the newsagent promises to write the house numbers on in future.

2 Unfortunately the next day the newsagent forgets to write the house numbers on the papers to be delivered to a block of three houses and again the paperboy has two papers to deliver. How many different ways could he deliver these two copies of *The Reflection*?

3 The very next day he has two unnumbered papers left to deliver to a court of four houses. How many different ways could he deliver these papers?

This became such a problem to him that he devised a system of setting out his problem using his own special notation. For example, if he had two papers left and five possible houses left he would write it as 2∗5. The value of 2∗5 is the number of different ways of delivering two papers to five houses.

4 What is the value of 2∗3, 2∗4, 2∗5, 2∗6? Write your results in a table.

Delivery problem	2∗3	2∗4	2∗5	2∗6	...
Number of different ways of delivering the papers (value)					

5 Work out the value of 2∗9.

6 Describe the sequence of the numbers in the bottom row of the table.

7 Find out the name of this sequence of numbers.

New York Cop and other investigations   37   © Cambridge University Press 1988

The paperboy's problem

This problem is not restricted to having two papers left.

8 Explain what 3*5 means.

9 What is the value of 3*5?

10 What is the connection between 2*5 and 3*5? Explain your answer.

11 What is the value of 1*5 and 4*5?

Obviously the value of 5*5 is 1 and by symmetry the value of 0*5 is also 1.

```
                        0*1    1*1
                   0*2    1*2    2*2
              0*3    1*3    2*3    3*3
         0*4    1*4    2*4    3*4    4*4
    0*5    1*5    2*5    3*5    4*5    5*5
```

This problem with the papers so interested the boy that after much research he found that if he set out his results in the form of a triangle (as shown above) he got an interesting pattern.

12 Replace the paperboy's notation in the triangle with the number of different ways of delivering the papers, that is the value number. (You have already worked out many of the values.)

13 Try to predict what the next line of the triangle will be.

14 What is the value of 5*9?

15 Find out the name of this triangular pattern of numbers.

New York Cop and other investigations

The paperboy's problem

Notes

Objectives
- To develop a systematic approach to the investigation and recording of a problem.
- To develop a sense of symmetry in a problem.
- To introduce the use of triangle numbers and Pascal's triangle into the solution of an investigation.
- (For the open investigation) To develop an effective system of notation.

Open investigation

Investigate the number of different ways in which two copies of the same newspaper can be delivered to five houses. It would not be sensible to deliver two copies of the same newspaper to the same house.

Extend this problem so that the number of newspapers to be delivered and the number of houses is varied.

Present your results in an orderly and systematic way.

Describe any connections between your results and any known sequences.

Range of ability

Age	Ability	100–	80–	60–40
13		4	–	–
14		11	4	–
15/16		Ext	15	11

Pre-knowledge Experience of more straightforward organisational investigation.

Equipment Normal classroom equipment.

Extensions Investigate the effect of using different newspapers so that it makes sense to deliver more than one newspaper to a house.

Solutions

1 10 different ways

2 3 different ways.

3 6

4

Delivery problem	2∗3	2∗4	2∗5	2∗6
Number of different ways of delivering the papers (value)	3	6	10	15

5 Continuing the pattern in the table.

```
2∗7    2∗8    2∗9
 21     28     36
```

6 The difference between consecutive numbers increases by 1 each time.

7 Triangle numbers

8 Three papers are left to deliver to five houses.

9 The value of 3∗5 is 10.

10 The values are the same. If 2 out of 5 houses have papers delivered to them, 3 out of 5 must not have papers; and vice versa.

11 The value of 1∗5 is 5 and so the value of 4∗5 must be 5.

12
```
            1    1
          1   2    1
       1    3    3    1
    1    4    6    4    1
 1    5   10   10    5    1
```

13 1 6 15 20 15 6 1

14 The value of 5∗9 is 126 (produced by extending the pattern in the triangle).

15 Pascal's triangle

New York Cop and other investigations © Cambridge University Press 1988

Number walls

1. Choose four different numbers and write them in any order in the bottom row of a 4 high wall on your worksheet.

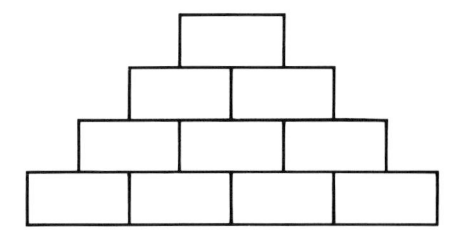

2. Add together the first two numbers on the bottom row and write the total in the brick above them.

3. Continue adding the numbers next to each other on the bottom row and writing the answer in the brick above.

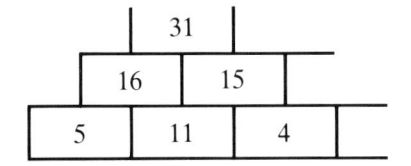

4. Carry on with this process up the wall until you get to the top row.

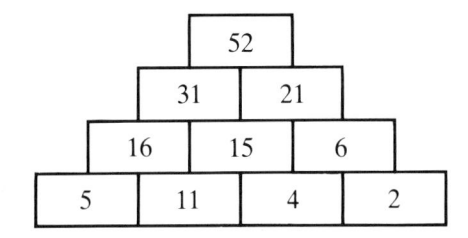

5. What is the number at the top of **your** wall?

6. On a new diagram of the wall write the same four starting numbers in the bottom row but put them in a different order. Complete the wall as before.

7. Was the number in the top brick the same as before?

8. Try other arrangements of the same four numbers in the bottom row. See what number you obtain in the top brick.

9. Can you see any similarity between some of the walls you have made? Explain what you notice.

10. Which of the arrangements give you the largest possible number in the top brick?

11. Which of the arrangements give you the smallest possible number in the top brick?

12. How would you arrange the numbers 3, 7, 11 and 14 in the bottom row of your wall to get the largest number in your top brick?

13. How would you arrange the numbers 3, 7, 11 and 14 in the bottom row of your wall to get the smallest number in your top brick?

14. Explain how you would arrange a set of any four numbers in the bottom row so that you obtain the largest number in the top brick.

15. Still using a 4 high wall, put the letters *A*, *B*, *C* and *D* in the bottom row. What will the top brick contain?

continued

New York Cop and other investigations   **41**   © Cambridge University Press 1988

Number walls

16 How would you arrange the numbers 2, 3, 4, 5, 6 in the bottom row of a 5 high wall to obtain the largest possible number in the top brick?

17 Using the letters A, B, C, D and E in the bottom row of a 5 high wall, find the contents of the top brick.

18 Investigate the contents for the top brick of walls of different sizes.

19 There is a pattern in the numbers in the top brick of different sized walls. Try to describe the pattern.

20 What will be the numbers in the top brick of a wall 8 bricks long, if you start off with A, B, C, D, E, F, G and H?

Number walls

Notes

Objectives
- To develop the ability to optimise in a numerical situation.
- To develop the ability to manipulate the use of letters to represent numbers.
- To introduce Pascal's triangle.

Open investigation Use the introduction as given in the structured investigation up to question 6 followed by:

7 Arrange a different set of numbers so that the number in the top brick is as large as possible. Explain how you would arrange any set of numbers in the bottom row so that the number in the top brick is as large as possible.

8 Instead of putting numbers in the bottom row, use the letters *A*, *B*, *C* and *D* in order. Using the same rule as before work out the expression that would be written in the top brick.

9 Follow the same pattern as in question 8 but use different sized walls. Write down the set of **numbers** (the coefficients of the terms) in the top brick. Arrange the sets of numbers in order and try to find a pattern. Describe any pattern you find.

Range of ability

	Ability	100–	80–	60–40
Age	13	15	15	15
	14	20	20	20
	15/16	Ext	/	/

Pre-knowledge An ability to add simple algebraic terms will make the final investigation more satisfactory.

Equipment A master for the walls is provided at the back of this book.

Extensions Instead of using a two-dimensional wall, use a tetrahedral pile of spheres. Name each sphere in the bottom layer with a letter. Name the sphere on the next layer above with the sum of the three spheres on which it rests.

Solutions

1, 2, 3, 4, 5, 6 Pupils will have different numbers at the top of their wall depending on their four starting numbers.

7 Most pupils will obtain a different number after changing the order of the four starting numbers.

8 The pupil's own arrangement.

9 Reflections will give the same answer.

10 To get the largest number in the top brick, the two largest starting numbers must be in the middle of the bottom row.

11 To get the smallest number in the top brick, the two smallest starting numbers must be in the middle of the bottom row.

12 11 and 14 will be in the middle of the bottom row.

13 3 and 7 will be in the middle.

14 The smallest two numbers must be in the outside bricks and the largest two numbers in the centre bricks.

43

15

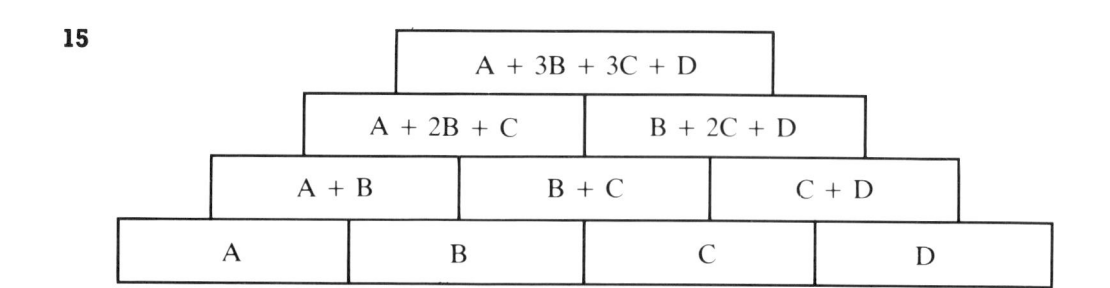

		A + 3B + 3C + D		
	A + 2B + C		B + 2C + D	
	A + B	B + C	C + D	
A	B	C	D	

16 2, 4, 6, 5, 3 or 2, 5, 6, 4, 3 or 3, 4, 6, 5, 2 or 3, 5, 6, 4, 2

17 $A + 4B + 6C + 4D + E$

18 The pupil's own investigation.

19 The coefficients of the letters in the nth row up will form the nth row of Pascal's triangle.

20 $A + 7B + 21C + 35D + 35E + 21F + 7G + H$

Door numbers

George Street is made up of two rows of houses. All the odd numbered houses (1, 3, 5, ...) are on one side of the street and all the even numbered houses (2, 4, 6, ...) are on the opposite side of the street.

The last house in the street is number 12.

1 What is the last odd number?

2 List all the numbers of the odd numbered houses in the street.

3 What is the sum of all these door numbers?

4 List all the numbers of the even numbered houses in the street.

5 What is the sum of all the even numbers in the street?

Albert Road is numbered in a similar way but the last house in the road is numbered 16.

6 What is the sum of all the odd door numbers in this road?

7 What is the sum of all the even door numbers in this road?

8 Copy and complete this table.

Street	Last house number	Number of houses down each side of street	Sum of the odd door numbers	Sum of the even door numbers
Henry Place	2			
Victoria Lane	4			
Charles Street	6			
Elizabeth Way	8			
Mary Road	10			
George Street	12			
Ann Way	14			
Albert Road	16			

The last house number on Brighouse Road is 50.

9 How many houses will there be on each side of the road?

10 What is the sum of the odd door numbers on this road?

11 What is the sum of the even door numbers on this road?

12 What would be the sum of the odd door numbers in a road which has n houses down both sides?

13 What would be the sum of the even door numbers in a road which has n houses down both sides?

New York Cop and other investigations

Door numbers

Notes

Objectives
- To develop an understanding of odd and even numbers.
- To develop an ability to find the sum of the first n odd and n even numbers.
- To recognise square numbers in unfamiliar situations.

Open investigation The sum of the first three odd numbers is 9 ($= 1 + 3 + 5$).

1. What is the sum of the first six odd numbers?

2. Extend the odd number sequence. What can you say about the sum of different lengths of this sequence, remembering to start from the first term each time?

3. What is the sum of the first n odd numbers?

The sum of the first three even numbers is 12 ($= 2 + 4 + 6$).

4. What is the sum of the first six even numbers?

5. Extend the even number sequence. What can you say about the sum of different lengths of this sequence, remembering to start from the first term each time?

6. What is the sum of the first n even numbers?

Range of ability

	Ability	100–	80–	60–40
Age	13	13	11	11
	14	Ext	Ext	13
	15/16	/	/	Ext

Pre-knowledge Understanding of odd, even and square numbers.

Equipment Usual classroom equipment.

Extensions Find the sum to n terms of other sequences; for example, counting numbers, multiples of 5, and square numbers.

Solutions

1. 11
2. 1, 3, 5, 7, 9, 11
3. 36
4. 2, 4, 6, 8, 10, 12
5. 42
6. 64
7. 72

8

Street	Last house number	Number of houses down each side of street	Sum of the odd door numbers	Sum of the even door numbers
Henry Place	2	1	1	2
Victoria Lane	4	2	4	6
Charles Street	6	3	9	12
Elizabeth Way	8	4	16	20
Mary Road	10	5	25	30
George Street	12	6	36	42
Ann Way	14	7	49	56
Albert Road	16	8	64	72

9   25

10   625

11   650

12 n^2

13 $n^2 + n$

Crossed lines

If you draw some straight lines on paper you can draw them so that they do or do not cross.

Three straight lines can be drawn so that the lines never cross each other.

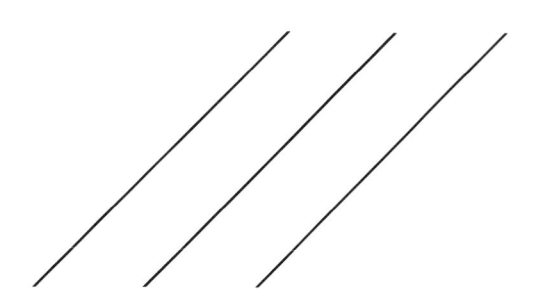

Or so that one line crosses the other two. (This arrangement has two crossing points.)

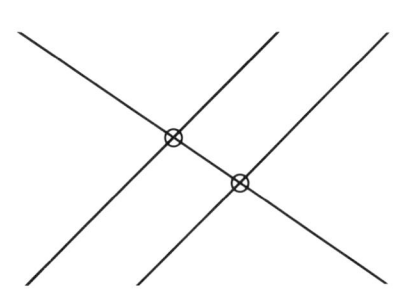

Or so that all three lines cross each other. (This arrangement has three crossing points.)

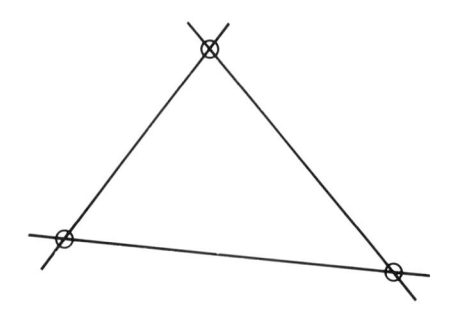

1 Lines which do not cross however far they are extended have a special name. What is it?

2 What is the maximum number of crossing points with five lines?

3 Copy and complete this table.

Number of lines	1	2	3	4	5	6	7	8
Maximum number of crossing points			3					

4 If ten lines were drawn so that they all crossed each other, how many crossing points would there be?

5 Now describe this pattern and write down a rule to give you the next number in the sequence, and explain why this works.

6 Find out the name of the sequence of numbers in the crossing points row.

7 If n lines were drawn so that they all crossed each other, what would be the maximum number of crossing points?

New York Cop and other investigations

Crossed lines

You can also investigate the number of regions formed by lines which all cross each other.

One line gives two regions.

The maximum number of regions formed by two lines is four.

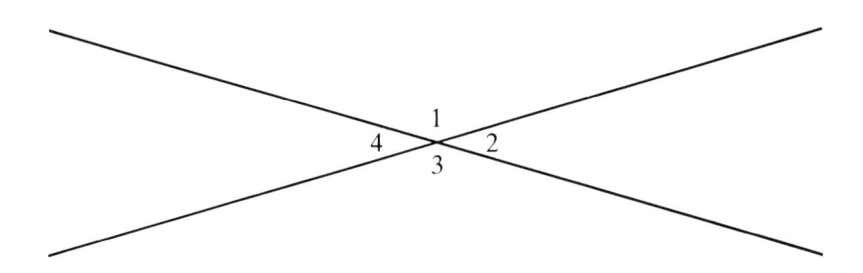

8 How many regions are formed when four lines are drawn so that they all cross?

9 Draw a table and continue until you find a pattern.

10 How many regions are formed when 15 lines are drawn so that they all cross each other?

11 Write down a rule to give you the next number in this sequence.

12 If n lines were drawn crossing each other, what is the number of regions formed?

13 What is the relationship between the number of crossing points and the number of regions?

Crossed lines

Notes

Objectives
- To develop knowledge of simple geometric properties.
- To develop the use and knowledge of triangle numbers.
- To develop knowledge of both inductive relationships and algebraic relationships.

Open investigation Use the introduction as given in the structured investigation up to question 2 followed by:

3 Develop the investigation so that you can predict the number of crossing points for any number of lines.

4 Write down the relationship between the number of lines and the number of crossing points.

Use the explanation from the structured investigation between questions 7 and 8.

5 Find the relationship between the number of lines and the number of regions formed.

Range of ability

	Ability	100–	80–	60–40
Age	13	7	6	6
	14	13	10	10
	15/16	Ext	13	11

Pre-knowledge Knowledge of triangle numbers is useful in this investigation.

Equipment Normal classroom equipment.

Extensions How many crossing points are produced when each dot in a row of n dots is joined to each dot in a parallel row of m dots?

Solutions

1 Parallel lines   2 10 crossings

3
Number of lines	1	2	3	4	5	6	7	8
Maximum number of crossing points	0	1	3	6	10	15	21	28

4 45 crossings with 10 lines

5 Number of crossing points = previous number of lines + previous number of crossing points.

Each new line must cross all the previous lines.

6 Triangle numbers   7 $\frac{1}{2}n(n-1)$ 8 11

9
Number of lines	1	2	3	4	5	6	7	8
Number of regions	2	4	7	11	16	22	29	37

10 121

11 Number of regions = previous number of regions + number of lines

12 $\frac{1}{2}n(n+1) + 1$

13 Number of crossing points + number of lines + 1 = number of regions

Rectangle mania

Here is a drawing of a rectangle split up by two parallel lines across its length. In the diagram there are more than three rectangles. The total number of rectangles is six. Two of the rectangles are ABCD and EFCD.

1. List the other four rectangles. Be careful not to write down the same one twice.

2. Draw a diagram to show a large rectangle split up by three parallel lines across the page. How many rectangles are in your diagram?

3. Do the same with four parallel lines across the page.

4. Copy and complete this table.

Number of lines across the page	0	1	2	3	4	5	6
Total number of rectangles			6				

5. What is the name of the sequence of numbers on the bottom row?

6. How many rectangles are formed using 11 parallel lines across one large rectangle?

7. How many rectangles are formed using n parallel lines across one large rectangle?

Instead of using parallel lines across the page you can split up the rectangle with lines running up the page.

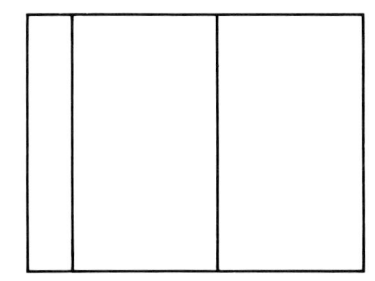

8. Copy and complete this table.

Number of lines up the page	0	1	2	3	4	5	6
Total number of rectangles			6				

9. Explain the connection between this table and the first table.

New York Cop and other investigations — 51 — © Cambridge University Press 1988

Rectangle mania

In this diagram a rectangle is split using two parallel lines across the page and one line up the page.

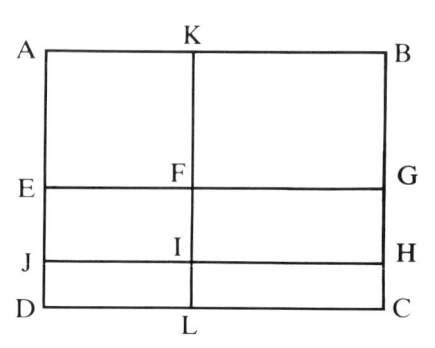

10 Make a list of all the rectangles in the diagram.

11 How many are there?

12 Look back at the two tables you have completed. Write down the connection between the number of rectangles formed; with one line up the page; with two lines across the page **and** with one line up the page and two lines across the page.

13 How many rectangles will be formed if you use two lines across and three lines up?

14 Explain how you can work out the total number of rectangles formed by six lines up the page and four lines across.

15 How many would this be?

16 Write a formula to calculate the total number of rectangles formed using m lines up the page and n lines across.

Rectangle mania

Notes

Objectives
- To develop the skill of careful systematic listing and recording.
- To introduce the sequence of triangle numbers.

Open investigation Use the introduction as given in the structured investigation up to question 2 followed by:

3 Work out the rule which will give the number of rectangles if n lines are drawn across the page.

4 If the rectangle is cut by lines across the page and lines up the page then the number of rectangles formed follows a different rule. Try to find this rule.

5 Write down a formula to describe the number of rectangles formed with n lines up and m lines across the page.

Range of ability

	Ability	100–	80–	60–40
Age	13	–	–	–
	14	12	12	–
	15/16	Ext	16	12

Pre-knowledge Some knowledge of algebra is needed for the last question.

Equipment Normal classroom equipment.

Extensions How many cuboids are formed when a large cuboid is divided by planes which run parallel to each pair of parallel faces?

Solutions

1 ABFE, ABGH, EFGH, HGCD

2 There are 10 rectangles in this diagram.

3 There are 15 rectangles in this diagram.

4
Number of lines across the page	0	1	2	3	4	5	6
Total number of rectangles	1	3	6	10	15	21	28

5 These are triangle numbers.

6 78

7 $\frac{1}{2}(n + 1)(n + 2)$

8

Number of lines up the page	0	1	2	3	4	5	6
Total number of rectangles	1	3	6	10	15	21	28

9 The two tables are the same because the original rectangle has been rotated through 90°.

10
AKFE   KBGF   EGHJ   IHCL
AKIJ   KBHI   EGCD
AKLD   KBCL   JHCD

ABGE   FGHI
ABHJ   EFIJ   FGCL
ABCD   EFLD
               JILD

(A systematic approach to listing should be encouraged.)

11 There are 18 in all.

12 (Number with 1 line up) × (Number with 2 lines across) = Number with 1 line up and 2 lines across.

13 6 × 10 = 60

14 (Number with 6 lines up) × (Number with 4 lines across) = Number with 6 lines up and 4 lines across.

15 28 × 15 = 420

16 $\frac{1}{2}(m+1)(m+2) \times \frac{1}{2}(n+1)(n+2) = \frac{1}{4}(m+1)(m+2)(n+1)(n+2)$

Hectic hockey

Almondbury	1	Brighouse	3	Brighouse	2
Brighouse	2	Cowlersley	2		
Cowlersley	4				
Deighton	1				
Fartown	0	Grove Street	0	Honley	1
Grove Street	3	Honley	4		
Honley	2				
Independents	1				

Helen Hirst, as Huddersfield Hockey League and Cup fixture secretary, has a problem. Thirty-two teams have entered the Huddersfield Hockey Knockout Competition. All the matches must be played on the same day and there is only limited time available. Helen has to work out the number of matches to be played so that she can work out the time allowed for each match.

1. Obviously two teams will be in the final round, but how many will be in the semi-final round?

2. How many teams will there be in the quarter-final round?

3. How many teams will have to be in the round before the quarter-final round?

4. How many rounds will have to be played to decide the cup winner out of Helen's 32 teams?

5. If a cup competition required just 7 full rounds to decide the winning team, how many teams must have entered the competition?

6. Copy and complete this table.

Number of rounds (r)	1	2	3	4	5	6	7
Number of teams (t)	2						

7. Work out the relationship between the number of rounds and the number of teams competing.

8. Write a formula which links the number of rounds (r) with the number of teams (t).

New York Cop and other investigations

Hectic hockey

Later on in the season ten teams enter the Huddersfield Cup so Helen has another problem. She decides to have a preliminary round to knock two teams out of the competition.

9 Why is it difficult to arrange a knockout competition for ten teams?

10 How many teams will have to play in the preliminary round?

11 How many rounds will there be in this competition (including the preliminary round)?

12 How many rounds will be needed for a competition in which 25 teams take part?

13 Explain how you would organise the matches for 25 teams. How many teams would be in the preliminary round?

Helen also needs to be able to work out the number of matches to be played assuming there are no replays.

14 If 4 teams entered a knockout competition, how many matches would have to be played?

15 If 16 teams entered a knockout competition, how many matches would have to be played.

16 If 25 teams entered a knockout competition, how many matches would have to be played?

17 What is the relationship between the number of teams entered and the number of matches played?

18 Explain your answer to the previous question.

Helen decides to try a league system and so she needs to know how many matches would have to be played in the league.

19 If 4 teams entered a league and each team played each other once only, how many matches would have to be played?

20 How many matches would have to be played if 5 teams entered the league?

21 Copy and complete this table.

Number of teams	2	3	4	5	6	7	8
Number of matches	1						

22 If 12 teams entered the league how many matches would have to be played?

23 How many matches would have to be played if n teams entered the league?

New York Cop and other investigations 56 © Cambridge University Press 1988

Hectic hockey

Notes

Objectives
- To show how to plan and construct a knockout competition and a league table.
- To develop knowledge of the sequence of 2^n.
- To develop knowledge of triangle numbers.

Open investigation It is difficult to bring out all the points raised in the structured investigation if this piece of work is presented as an open investigation. It may well be better to set this as a class exercise so that the problems inherent in the investigation can be brought out by class discussion.

Range of ability

Age	Ability	100–	80–	60–40
13		–	–	–
14		23	23	–
15/16		23	23	23

Pre-knowledge This investigation uses a lot of terms that may not be familiar to all members of the class. The idea of a knockout competition and a league should be discussed before starting.

Equipment Normal classroom equipment.

Extensions This is a self-contained piece of work.

Solutions

1. 4 teams
2. 8 teams
3. 16 teams
4. 5 rounds
5. 128 teams
6.

Number of rounds (r)	1	2	3	4	5	6	7
Number of teams (t)	2	4	8	16	32	64	128

7. With every extra round added twice as many teams are required. The number of teams required is a power of 2.
8. $t = 2^r$
9. With 10 teams if you have a simple knockout competition you will have 5 teams in the second round – this will not divide by 2.
10. 4
11. 4
12. 5

13 The preliminary round must knock out 9 teams, so 18 teams must play in the preliminary round.

Preliminary round	18 → 9 winners
1st round	9 + 7 = 16
Quarter-final	8
Semi-final	4
Final	2

14 4 teams require 3 matches.

15 16 teams require 15 matches.

16 25 teams require 24 matches.

17 The number of matches is one less than the number of teams entered.

18 Every team but the winners must lose one and only one match.

19 4 teams require 6 matches.

20 5 teams require 10 matches.

21

Number of teams	2	3	4	5	6	7	8
Number of matches	1	3	6	10	15	21	28

22 12 teams require 66 matches.

23 $\frac{1}{2}n(n-1)$

Chequered flags

This diagram represents a 4 by 6 chequered flag made up from black and white squares. Notice that there is a black square in the top left-hand corner.

1. How many squares are used altogether to make this flag?
2. How many squares are black?
3. Draw a 4 by 5 chequered flag. Always start with a black square in the top left-hand corner.
4. How many of the squares on a 4 by 5 chequered flag are white?
5. In a 20 by 25 chequered flag, how many squares are black and how many are white?
6. In an m by n chequered flag, how many squares are black and how many are white?

This diagram shows a 5 by 7 chequered flag.

7. How many black squares are there on this flag?
8. How many white squares are there on this flag?
9. Does the formula you found for question 6 work for a 5 by 7 flag?
10. What can you say about the dimension of a flag for which the rule in question 6 does work?
11. Explain your answer.

This diagram represents a 3 by 5 flag.

12. How many squares are there altogether in a 3 by 5 flag?
13. How many squares are black and how many are white?
14. How many squares are there on a 21 by 29 flag?
15. How many squares are black and how many are white?
16. How many squares are black and how many are white in an m by n chequered flag where m and n are both odd?

New York Cop and other investigations © Cambridge University Press 1988

Chequered flags

Notes

Objectives
- To develop an understanding of multiplying odd and even numbers.
- To show that some solutions to problems are disjoint.
- To recognise and construct simple relationships between two variables.

Open investigation Use the introduction as given in the structured investigation up to question 2 followed by:

3 In a 20 by 25 chequered flag, how many squares are black and how many are white?

4 In a 3 by 5 chequered flag, how many squares are there altogether? How many are black and how many are white? (Be careful!)

5 In a 21 by 29 chequered flag, how many squares are black and how many are white?

6 In an n by m chequered flag, how many squares are black and how many are white? State clearly to which situations your formulas apply.

Range of ability

Ability	100–	80–	60–40
Age 13	16	15	–
14	Ext	16	15
15/16	/	Ext	16

Pre-knowledge
- Awareness of the concept of odd and even numbers.
- Ability to construct simple formulas.

Equipment Squared paper.

Extensions Three-coloured flags. How many A, B, C squares are there in n by m chequered flags?

A	B	C	A	B
C	A	B	C	A
B	C	A	B	C

Solutions

1 24

2 12

3

4   10

5   250 black and 250 white

6   $\frac{1}{2}mn$ black, $\frac{1}{2}mn$ white!

7   18

8   17

9   No. The formula in question 6 does not work.

10 The number of squares in the flag must be even. So either the length or width (or both) must be even.

11 If the total number of squares is even then the total number of squares can be divided by 2 to give the same number of black and white squares.

12 15

13 8 black, 7 white

14 609

15 305 black, 304 white

16 $\frac{1}{2}(mn+1)$ black, $\frac{1}{2}(mn-1)$ white

Cutting corners

A cube has 6 faces
12 edges
8 vertices or corners.

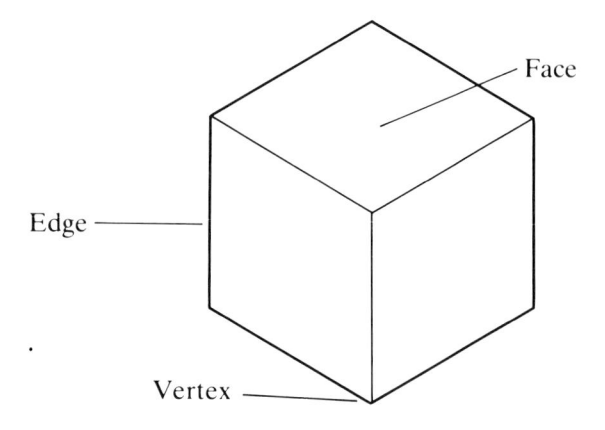

The vertices can be chopped off to make a 'truncated cube'. A truncated cube has more faces, vertices and edges than the original cube.

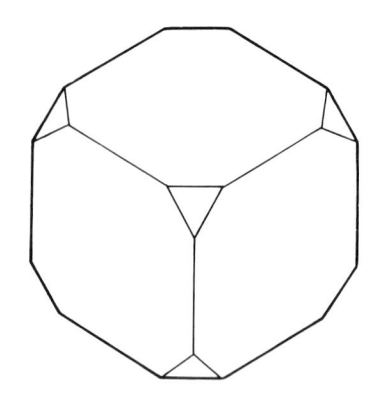

1 Work out how many faces (*F*), vertices (*V*) and edges (*E*) a solid has which is formed from a cube with only **one** vertex chopped off.

2 Suppose a cube has two of its vertices chopped off. What shape is each new face? Is this always true?

3 How many edges, faces and vertices does this new solid have?

Record your result in a table.

Number of vertices chopped from cube	Number of faces, *F*	Number of vertices, *V*	Number of edges, *E*
0	6	8	12
1			

4 Continue the table by chopping off more of the original vertices of the cube.

5 Find a relationship between *V*, *F* and *E*.

New York Cop and other investigations — © Cambridge University Press 1988

Cutting corners

You can chop off the vertices of an octahedron in a similar way.

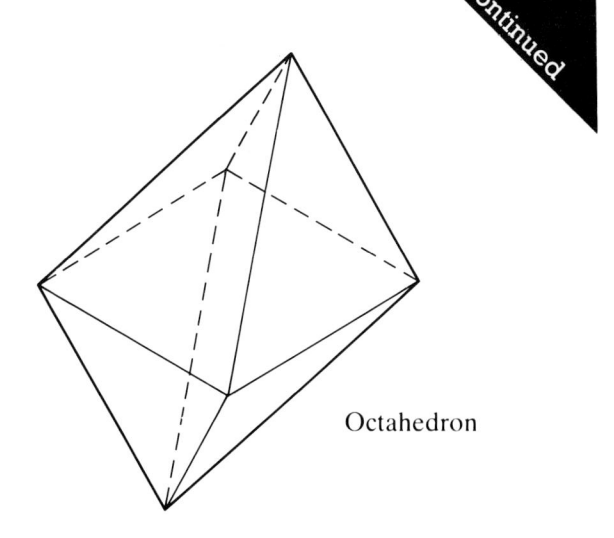

Octahedron

6 Draw up a table similar to that for the cube and complete it for the faces, edges and vertices of an octahedron.

7 Does the relationship you found for the cube-solids work for the octahedron-solids?

8 Try other solids and check your relationship each time.

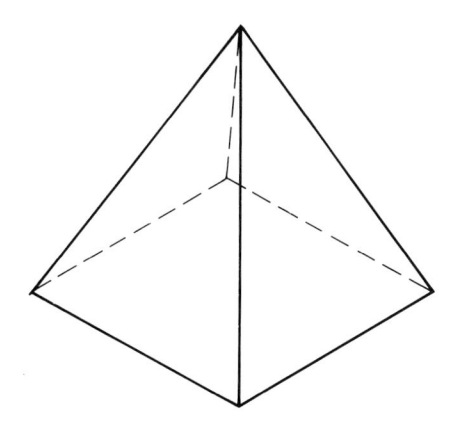

Square-based pyramid

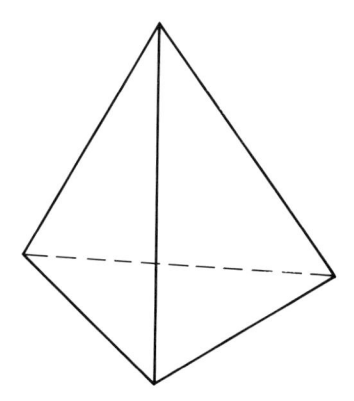

Tetrahedron

New York Cop and other investigations

Cutting corners

Notes

Objectives
- To reinforce knowledge of solid shapes.
- To develop a sense of spatial awareness.
- To develop use of simple algebraic relationships.

Open investigation Use the introduction used in the structured investigation followed by:

1. If you cut off one vertex of a cube, how many faces, vertices and edges has the new shape?

2. Construct a table of results recording the number of faces, vertices and edges for the new solid made as successive corners are cut off.

3. Find a relationship between the number of faces, vertices and edges which is correct no matter how many corners are cut off.

4. Find the relationship between the number of faces, vertices and edges for other solids.

Range of ability

	Ability	100–	80–	60–40
Age	13	8	–	–
	14	8	8	4
	15/16	Ext	8	8

Pre-knowledge Pupils need to know the names and nature of the most common solids.

Equipment
- Models of the solids under investigation would be useful.
- Modelling clay can be used to demonstrate the effect of cutting off a vertex but is not suitable for the pupils to use in the investigation as the solid soon becomes a sphere!

Extensions This can be extended to other solids and using other types of cuts. For example, a V cut can be taken out of one face.

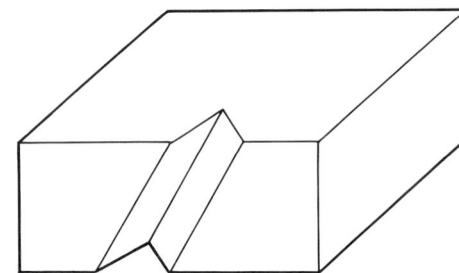

Solutions

1. $F = 7$, $V = 10$, $E = 15$

2. Triangular – yes, it is always true.

3. $F = 8$, $V = 12$, $E = 18$

4.

Number of vertices chopped from cube	Number of faces, F	Number of vertices, V	Number of edges, E
0	6	8	12
1	7	10	15
2	8	12	18
3	9	14	21
4	10	16	24

5 $F + V - 2 = E$

6

Number of vertices chopped from octahedron	F	V	E
0	8	6	12
1	9	9	16
2	10	12	20
3	11	15	24
4	12	18	28

7 This relationship holds for any solid shape.

8 Tetrahedron

Number of vertices chopped from tetrahedron	F	V	E
0	4	4	6
1	5	6	9
2	6	8	12
3	7	10	15
4	8	12	18

NB. The order in which the vertices are cut off a square-based pyramid will affect the results table but the relationship will always hold.

A cube investigation

If you use red paint to paint the outside of a three centimetre cube and then cut it up into single centimetre cubes as shown in the diagram, you will have unit cubes that have different numbers of their faces painted.

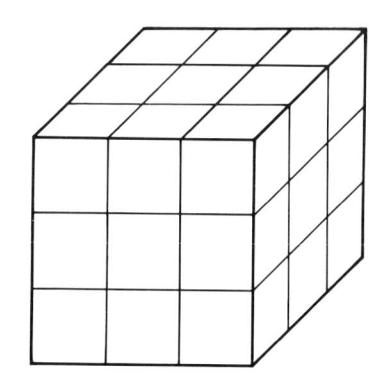

1. How many unit cubes will there be?

   This unit cube has three faces painted red. The other three faces are unpainted but you cannot see them. We will call this type of unit cube a type A cube.

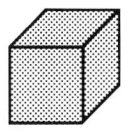

2. How many type A cubes will there be, and what can you say about their position in the large cube?

   Some unit cubes will have two faces painted red. We will call these type B cubes.

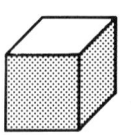

3. How many type B cubes will there be, and where will you find them in the large cube?

4. How many unit cubes will have just one face painted? We will call these type C cubes.

5. How many cubes will have no red faces? These will be called type D cubes.

6. As the size of the cube is changed (4 cm, 5 cm, 6 cm, ...), what happens to the number of type A cubes in it when it is cut up? Does it matter to the number of type A cubes how big you make the large cube? Why?

7. Investigate what happens to the number of type B cubes as the size of the painted cube changes. Record your results under these headings:

Length of side (L)	Number of type B cubes (B)
2	
3	
4	
5	

8. Write down a rule that links L to B.

9. The number of type C cubes also changes as the size of the painted cube changes. Look at this problem and record your results under these headings:

Length of side (L)	Number of type C cubes (C)
2	
3	
4	
5	

10. Write down the rule that links L to C.

New York Cop and other investigations

A cube investigation

The type D cubes are more difficult because you cannot see them but they are still there!

11 If the large cube is 4 by 4 by 4 cm, how many type D cubes are there?

12 What shape will the type D cubes always make, inside the painted cube?

13 Continue to investigate the type D cubes and record your results:

Length of side (L)	Number of type D cubes (D)
2	
3	
4	
5	

14 Write down the rule that links L to D.

15 If you have reached this far you should be able to write a rule that links L to A, B, C and D. Try to write it down in one big formula.

16 If a cube has 64 type D cubes, how many unit cubes does it have altogether?

17 If another cube has 60 type B cubes, how many type C cubes will it have?

A cube investigation

Notes

Objectives
- To develop an awareness of three-dimensional objects and the relationship between length, area and volume of a cube.
  To reinforce knowledge of edges, vertices and faces.
- To develop simple algebraic relationships.
- To make pupils aware that there are constraints to some solutions to a problem.

Open investigation Use the introduction as given in the structured investigation up to question 5 followed by:

6 Investigate how the number of each type of unit cube changes as the size of the original cube changes.

7 Record your results and try to find a relationship between the length of side of the original cube and the number of each type of unit cube.

8 Questions 16 and 17 of the structured investigation.

Range of ability

	Ability	100–	80–	60–40
Age	13	17	–	–
	14	17	–	–
	15/16	Ext	17	17

Most benefit is gained from this investigation when pupils have the ability to complete the major part of the work.

Pre-knowledge No specific requirements are needed for this investigation but a knowledge of square and cube numbers is an advantage.

Equipment A large supply of cubes.

Extensions Replace the cube by a triangular prism.

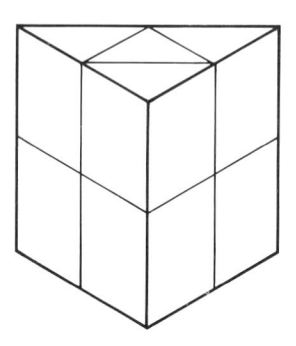

Solutions

1 27

2 8. They are at the vertices.

3 12. They are along the edges of the cube, excluding corners.

4 6 (found in the centre of each face)

5 1 (found in the centre of the large cube)

6 There will always be 8 as a cube always has 8 corners.

7

L	B
2	0
3	12
4	24
5	36

8 $B = 12(L - 2)$

9

L	C
2	0
3	6
4	24
5	54

10 $C = 6(L - 2)^2$

11 8

12 A cube

13

L	D
2	0
3	1
4	8
5	27

14 $D = (L - 2)^3$

15 $L^3 = A + B + C + D$

16 216

17 150

Around the garden

Rose Bush is a landscape gardener. She has to prepare flower beds in which to display her various blooms. The basic shape of the flower beds is square although she can join beds edge to edge to make larger beds and give the display variety.

For example   but not

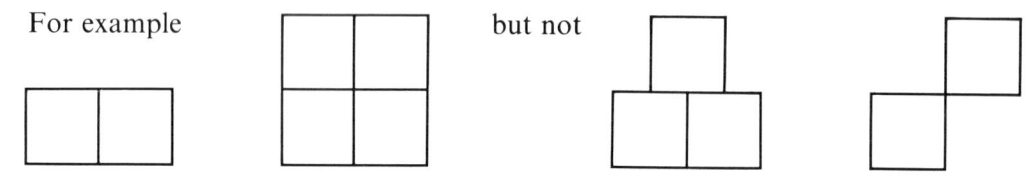

Many people are expected to visit the display. In order that as many people as possible can see the flowers she has to make the perimeter (the distance all the way round the outside of the beds) as large as possible.

This flower bed is made up of 7 squares and has a perimeter of 12.

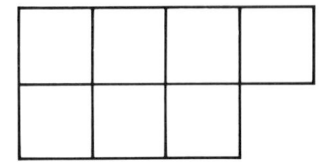

1 Draw another arrangement of these 7 square beds which will give a larger perimeter.

2 What is the maximum perimeter of a flower bed made up of 7 square beds?

3 What is the maximum perimeter of a flower bed made up of 9 square beds?

4 Copy and complete this table.

Number of square beds joined	1	2	3	4	5	6	7	8	9
Largest possible perimeter									

5 What would be the largest possible perimeter of a flower bed made up from 25 square beds?

6 What would be the largest possible perimeter of a flower bed made up from n square beds?

New York Cop and other investigations   70   © Cambridge University Press 1988

Around the garden

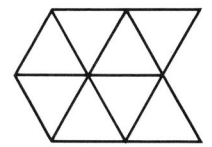

This bed is made up from 8 equilateral triangle shaped beds and has a perimeter of 8.

Rose still wishes to have the perimeter of the beds as large as possible.

7 Find a better arrangement for these 8 triangular beds which will give the largest possible perimeter.

8 Copy and complete this table.

Number of triangular beds	1	2	3	4	5	6
Largest possible perimeter						

9 What would be the largest possible perimeter of a bed made up from 25 equilateral triangular beds?

10 What would be the largest possible perimeter of a bed made up from n equilateral triangular beds?

Rose still isn't satisfied and so decides to build some regular hexagonal flower beds.

This bed is made up from 3 regular hexagonal beds and has a perimeter of 12.

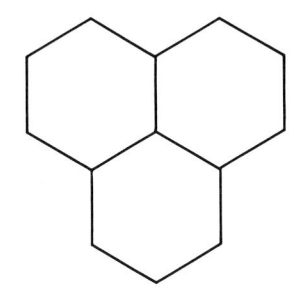

11 Copy and complete this table.

Number of hexagonal beds	1	2	3	4	5	6
Largest possible perimeter						

12 What would be the largest possible perimeter of a bed made up from n regular hexagons?

13 What would be the largest possible perimeter of a bed made up from n regular decagons?

14 What would be the largest possible perimeter of a bed made up from n regular polygon beds each with s sides?

New York Cop and other investigations © Cambridge University Press 1988

Around the garden

Notes

Objectives
- To develop the understanding of maximisation in the context of area and perimeter.
- To find simple relationships.
- To develop a more complex relationship from a series of simple relationships.

Open investigation

Squares can be put together edge to edge like this to give a shape which has a perimeter of 10.

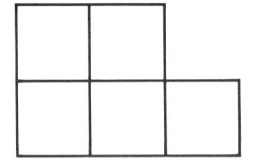

Shapes like these are not allowed. The squares must fit together edge to edge.

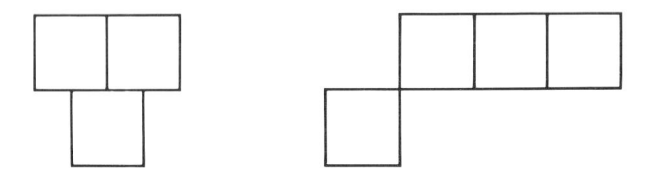

1. If you join 5 squares together edge to edge, what is the largest possible perimeter?

2. If 25 squares are joined together edge to edge, what is the largest possible perimeter?

3. If n squares are joined together edge to edge what is the largest possible perimeter?

This diagram shows 7 equilateral triangles joined together with a perimeter of 7.

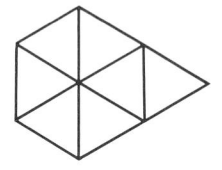

4. If n equilateral triangles are joined together edge to edge, what is the largest possible perimeter?

This diagram shows 3 regular hexagons joined together with a perimeter of 12.

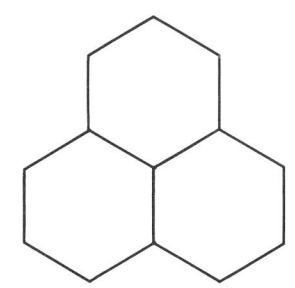

5. If n regular hexagons are joined together edge to edge, what is the largest possible perimeter?

6. If n regular shaped polygons with s sides are joined together edge to edge, what is the largest possible perimeter?

Range of ability

	Ability	100–	80–	60–40
Age	13	14	10	10
	14	Ext	14	14
	15/16	Ext	Ext	Ext

Pre-knowledge
- Understanding of perimeter.
- Ability to formulate simple two variable relationships.
- Understanding the terms square, equilateral triangle, hexagon, decagon and regular polygon.

Equipment Squared paper, isometric paper or triangular spotty paper. (A master for triangular spotty paper is provided at the back of this book.)

Extensions
1. Pentiles: How many different shapes can be made by putting 5 squares edge to edge? Look at the different ways of arranging 2, 3, 4, ... squares edge to edge.
2. Minimum perimeters by putting squares, triangles and hexagons together edge to edge. (Use only shapes that will tessellate.)

Solutions

1. Perimeter is 14 or 16. There are many solutions. One way to check diagrams is to use the relationship $P = 16 - 2n$ where P is the perimeter and n is the number of places where 4 squares meet.

2. 16

3. 20

4.
Number of square beds joined	1	2	3	4	5	6	7	8	9
Largest possible perimeter	4	6	8	10	12	14	16	18	20

5. 52

6. $2n+2$

7. Perimeter 10

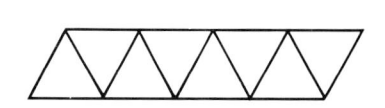

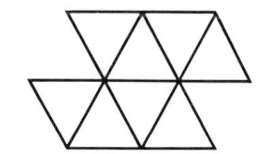

8.
Number of triangular beds	1	2	3	4	5	6
Largest possible perimeter	3	4	5	6	7	8

9. 27

10. $n+2$

11.
Number of hexagonal beds	1	2	3	4	5	6
Largest possible perimeter	6	10	14	18	22	26

12. $4n+2$

13. $8n+2$

14. $(s-2)n + 2$

Areas and perimeters

Shapes can be drawn on squared spotty paper with one dot inside.

This shape has 4 dots on the perimeter and has an area of 2 units.

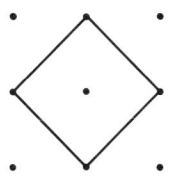

This shape has 7 dots on the perimeter and has an area of $3\frac{1}{2}$ units.

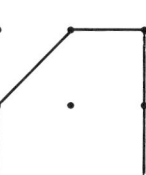

1 Draw different shapes with one dot inside and record your results in a table like the one below.

Number of dots on perimeter	3	4	5	6	7	8
Area of shape		2			$3\frac{1}{2}$	

2 What is the area of a shape with one dot inside which has 20 dots on the perimeter?

3 What is the area of a shape with one dot inside which has p dots on the perimeter?

Shapes can be drawn with no dots inside.

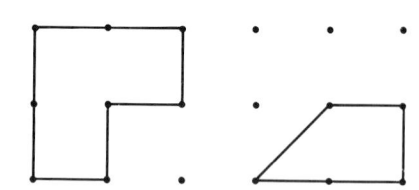

4 Copy and complete this table for shapes with no dots inside.

Number of dots on perimeter	3	4	5	6	7	8
Area of shape						

5 What is the area of a shape with no dots inside which has 20 dots on the perimeter?

6 What is the area of a shape with no dots inside which has p dots on the perimeter?

7 What is the area of a shape with 2 dots inside which has p dots on the perimeter?

8 What is the area of a shape with 3 dots inside which has p dots on the perimeter?

9 What is the area of a shape with 20 dots inside which has p dots on the perimeter?

10 Find the relationship between A, the area of a shape, d, the number of dots inside, and p, the number of dots on the perimeter.

Areas and perimeters

Notes

Objectives
- To develop the skill of calculating the area of complex shapes on a square lattice.
- To develop the skill of constructing simple and more complex formulas.

Open investigation

This shape has 1 dot inside,
4 dots on the perimeter
and has an area of 2 units.

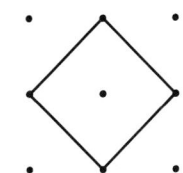

1. Look at other shapes drawn on square spotty paper which have 1 dot inside. Find a relationship which links their area to the number of dots on the perimeter.

   This shape has no dots inside.

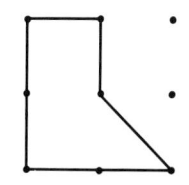

2. Find a relationship which links the area of shapes that have no dots inside to the number of dots on the perimeter.

3. Find relationships between the area A of shapes with 2, 3, 4, 5, ..., d dots inside and p dots on the perimeter.

Range of ability

Age	Ability	100–	80–	60–40
	13	9	9	–
	14	10	10	6
	15/16	Ext	Ext	10

Pre-knowledge
- An understanding of the defining of lengths in 'units', not simply cm, m etc.
- Ability to construct simple two-variable formulas, e.g. $d = 3l - 1$ from a table of results.
- Ability to recognise three-variable formulas, e.g. $d = 2wl + 1$

Equipment A master for squared spotty paper is provided at the back of this book.

Extensions Similar relationships for shapes made on triangular spotty paper using the equilateral triangle as the basic unit of area.

Solutions

1.
Number of dots on perimeter	3	4	5	6	7	8
Area of shape	$1\frac{1}{2}$	2	$2\frac{1}{2}$	3	$3\frac{1}{2}$	4

2. 10

3. $A = \frac{1}{2}p$

4

Number of dots on perimeter	3	4	5	6	7	8
Area of shape	$\frac{1}{2}$	1	$1\frac{1}{2}$	2	$2\frac{1}{2}$	3

5 9

6 $A = \frac{1}{2}p - 1$

7 $A = \frac{1}{2}p + 1$

8 $A = \frac{1}{2}p + 2$

9 $A = \frac{1}{2}p + 19$

10 $A = \frac{1}{2}p + d - 1$

Brighouse market

This diagram shows part of a plan of Brighouse market. The stalls are square shaped and are arranged in rows. The entrance to the market is at the top left hand corner (as indicated by *).

Suppose you were in a hurry because you had to meet a friend at the place marked with an X (at the junction of four stalls). You would obviously take one of the shortest routes. The diagram indicates one such route. This route is the length of 3 stalls.

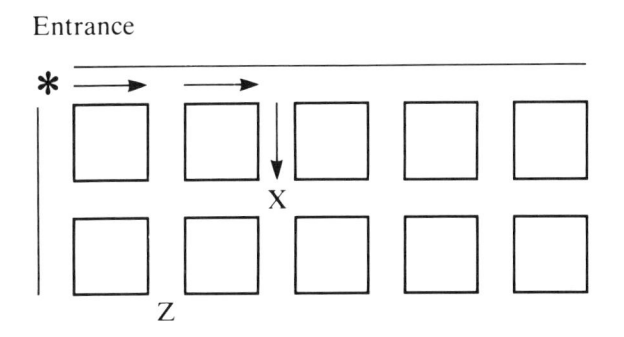

1. How many different routes are there from the entrance to X which are of the same '3 stall' length?

2. How many different ways are there of walking from the entrance to Z by the shortest route?

3. What do you notice about your answers to questions 1 and 2? Explain why this happens.

Now start with a simpler problem. If you look at just one bit of the market and you want to travel from * to A then the journey would be one stall long and there will only be one shortest route.

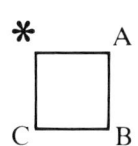

4. How many shortest routes are there from * to B? This is a journey of 2 stalls.

This is a larger part of the plan.

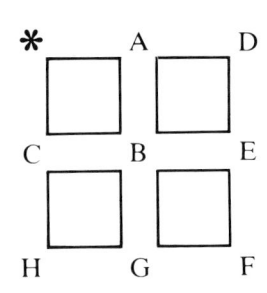

5. Work out the number of shortest possible routes from * to D.

6. Copy the diagram but replace the letters by the number of shortest possible routes from * to that letter. You have already worked out the shortest possible routes from * to A, B, C, D, E, G and H.

New York Cop and other investigations © Cambridge University Press 1988

Brighouse market

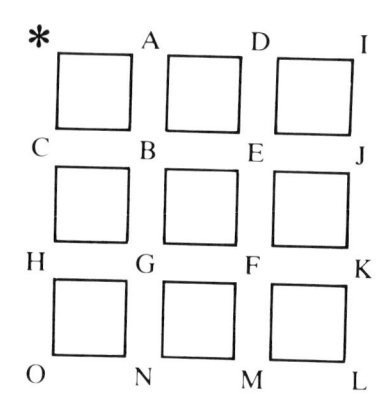

7 Now extend your diagram so that you have a 3 by 3 arrangement of stalls as shown in the diagram above, but do not write in the letters at the junctions.

Work out the shortest possible routes to each of the junctions and replace the letter by the number of shortest possible routes.

8 Extend your diagram so that you have a 4 by 4 arrangement of stalls. Write in the number of shortest routes at each of your new junctions.

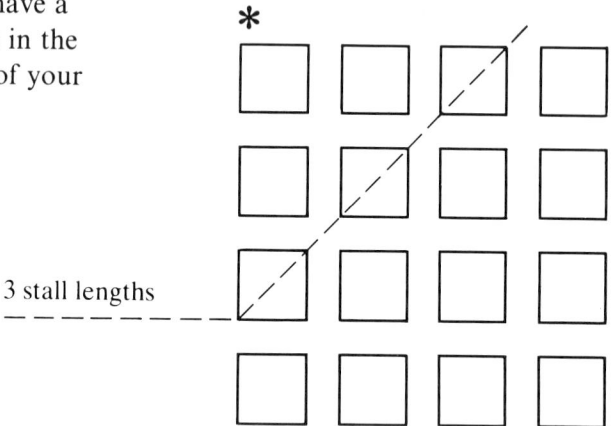

3 stall lengths

9 A dashed line has been drawn through the junctions that are 3 stall lengths away from the entrance *.

On your diagram draw a similar line through all the junctions which are 2 stall lengths from *. Label this line. Continue with this until you have connected all the junctions with labelled lines.

10 Can you see the pattern of the number of shortest possible routes to the junctions as the distance from * becomes greater? It may help if you rewrite your results like this

```
      C  A          1 stall length
   H  B  D          2 stall length
O  G  E  I          3 stall length
```

and replace the letter by the number of shortest possible routes.

11 Look at the results of the shortest journeys of lengths 1, 2, 3, 4, 5, ... (l). Add together the total number of different shortest journeys (t), that can be made for each journey length.

12 Can you see the connection between l and t?

New York Cop and other investigations

78

© Cambridge University Press 1988

Brighouse market

Notes

Objectives
- To develop a sense of symmetry in the solution of problems.
- To develop a systematic approach to solving spatial problems.
- To develop an awareness of Pascal's triangle.

Open investigation The same introduction as the structured investigation followed by:

Investigate how many different routes there are for journeys of the same length. Consider how this number changes as the length of the journey increases. Try to find a pattern to the number of routes as the journey length changes.

Range of ability

Ability	100–	80–	60–40
Age 13	–	–	–
14	12	–	–
15/16	Ext	12	9

Pre-knowledge No specific knowledge required but this is not suitable for pupils new to investigations.

Equipment
- Normal classroom equipment.
- A master providing blanks of the market is available at the back of this book.

Extensions Expand $(x+1)^2$, $(x+1)^3$, $(x+1)^4$, ... Can you predict the expansion of $(x+1)^n$? Explain your answer.

Solutions

1. 3
2. 3
3. They are the same because of the symmetry of the situation.
4. 2
5. 1
6.

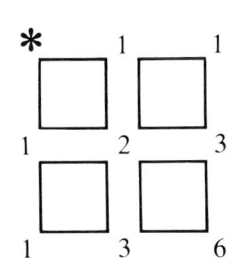

```
*     1    1
      □    □
 1    2    3
      □    □
 1    3    6
```

7.

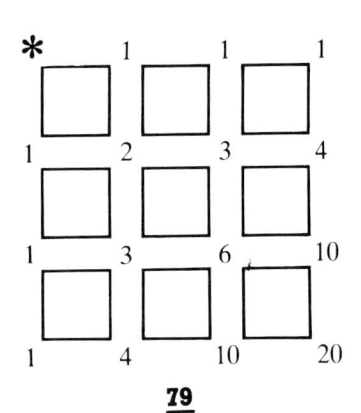

```
*     1    1    1
      □    □    □
 1    2    3    4
      □    □    □
 1    3    6   10
      □    □    □
 1    4   10   20
```

8, 9

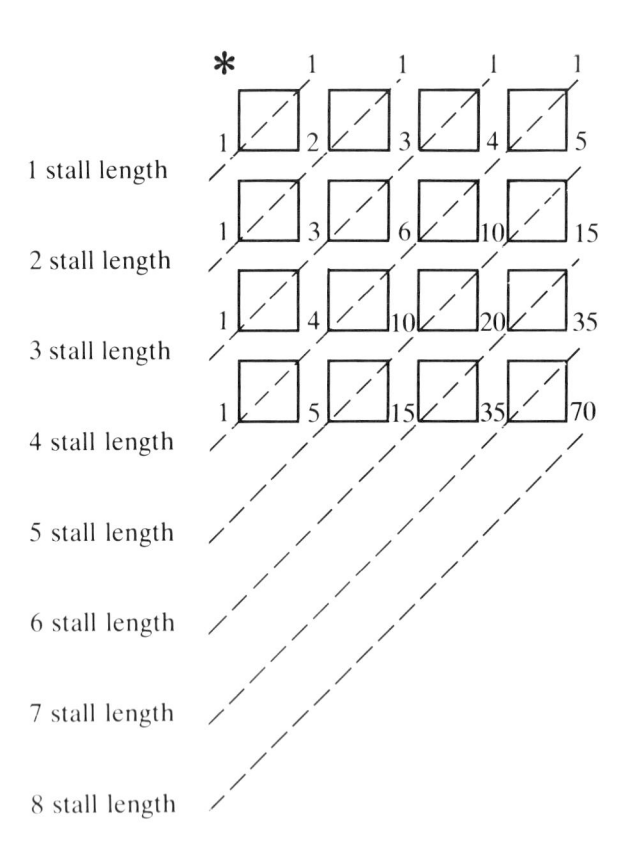

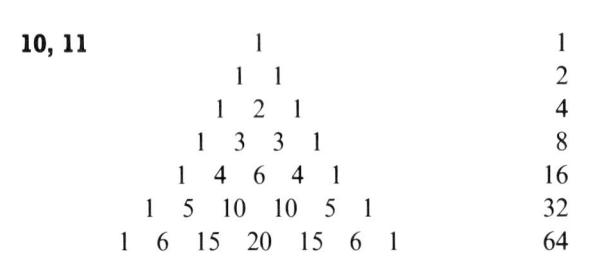

```
        *    1      1      1      1
         ▱     ▱     ▱     ▱
        1  2  3  4  5
1 stall length
         ▱     ▱     ▱     ▱
        1  3  6  10 15
2 stall length
         ▱     ▱     ▱     ▱
        1  4  10 20 35
3 stall length
         ▱     ▱     ▱     ▱
        1  5  15 35 70
4 stall length

5 stall length

6 stall length

7 stall length

8 stall length
```

10, 11

```
              1                      1
            1   1                    2
          1   2   1                  4
        1   3   3   1                8
      1   4   6   4   1             16
    1   5  10  10   5   1           32
  1   6  15  20  15   6   1         64
```

12 $t = 2^l$

New York Cop

The street system in New York is built up of blocks, and is in a rectangular array. The New York Police Department likes to have total supervision of all streets using as few officers as possible. A police officer can see all that is happening down the length of one block, but cannot see past a road junction.

A police officer standing at A can recognise villains in the region shown by the dotted lines. An officer at B can only survey two sides of a block, while officer C can cover three sides.

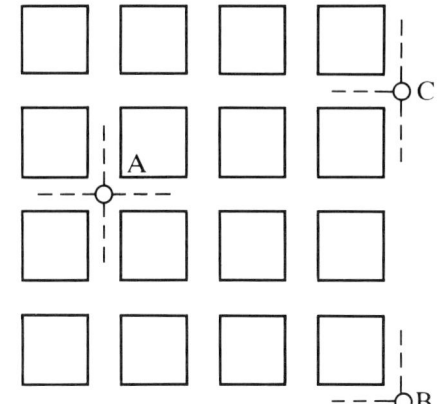

To police a particular row the captain places officers in the following places.

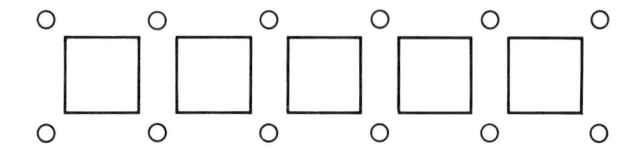

1. Are all these officers necessary to police this row?

2. Find a better arrangement that requires fewer officers and draw it. Make sure your arrangement uses the least possible number of officers to cover all the streets.

3. If the captain wants to police this row, what is the minimum number of officers required? (Remember you have to cover the outside.)

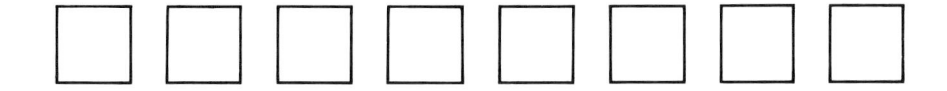

4. How many officers are needed to police a row of length 20 blocks?

5. Try to write a statement which describes how the captain can work out the number of officers needed to cover a row of any length.

6. Using p for the number of police officers and l for the length of the row, write down a formula which links p and l.

New York Cop and other investigations © Cambridge University Press 1988

New York Cop

The police captain finds that the officers have done their job so well that the villains are moving onto the streets either side of the original row.

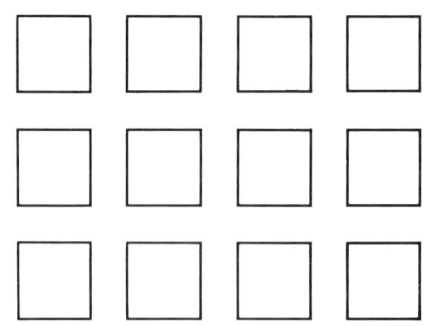

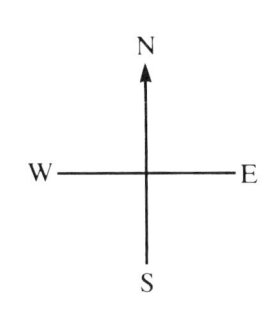

7 Show where the captain can best place some officers to cover the new zone.

8 If the zone to be policed is extended two more columns to the east, how many police officers would now be required?

9 Try to find a general statement to work out the number of police officers required to cover a precinct three blocks wide and of any length.

10 Using p for the number of police officers and l for the length of the row, write down a formula which links p and l.

11 Now try the same exercise with precincts that are 5, 7, 9, ..., w blocks wide.

12 Explain why the captain can use a formula to work out the number of officers required to police a zone when the width is an even number of blocks and the length is an odd number of blocks.

The captain finds that the rule for working out the number of officers does not work when the precinct is only two blocks wide and the length is an even number of blocks.

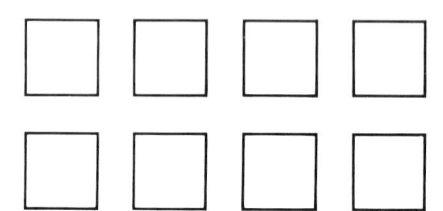

13 Try to find a rule which will help the captain to use the minimum number of officers to cover a precinct two blocks wide and a length l. Make sure you use the most efficient use of the officers.

14 Now do the same for precincts that are 4, 6, 8 blocks wide.

15 All you have to do to solve the captain's problems is to find a general rule for the numbe of police p required to cover a precinct w blocks wide and l blocks long when both l and w are even numbers.

New York Cop and other investigations © Cambridge University Press 1988

New York Cop

Notes

Objectives
- To develop the skill of optimisation.
- To recognise and construct a simple relationship between two variables.
- To construct compound relationships between three variables.
- To recognise that some solutions to problems are disjoint.

Open investigation The same introduction to the problem followed by:

1. How many officers would be required to police a single row of blocks of length l?
2. How many officers would be required to police three rows of blocks of length l?
3. Find the rule which gives the number of officers required to police any odd number of rows of length l.
4. Find a rule which connects the number of officers (n) required to police any even by even array of blocks l by w.

Range of ability

	Ability	100–	80–	60–40
Age	13	–	–	–
	14	11	10	–
	15/16	Ext	12	–

Pre-knowledge
- Use of algebraic expressions.
- Manipulation of algebraic expressions.

Equipment A master for diagrams of the blocks is provided at the back of this book.

Extensions Investigate the effect of an officer being able to see up to two block lengths in any direction instead of just one block.

Investigate the number of streets of unit length in a precinct l by w.

Solutions

1. No

2. The best solution is to place the officers as shown.

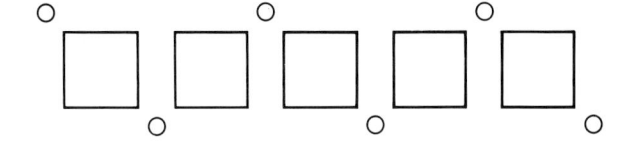

3. This requires 9 officers.

4. For 20 blocks 21 officers are required.

5.
l	p
5	6
8	9
20	21
l	$\rightarrow$ $l+1$

   The number of officers is one more than the number of blocks.

6. $p = l + 1$

   With less able pupils it may be better to avoid using algebraic equations.

7 Make sure at this point that the pupils have got a systematic and correct way of deploying officers.

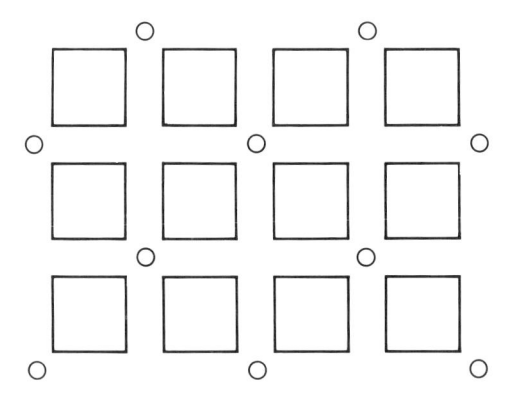

8 14 officers

9 For every row you need 2 officers plus 2.

10 For three rows

l	p
4	10
5	12
6	14
7	16
l →	$2l+2$

Again with less able children if they cannot use this form of description, encourage a verbal statement like:

'You need two extra police officers for every extra row.'

11 For five rows

l	p
1	6
2	9
3	12
4	15
l →	$3l+3$

For seven rows

l → $4l+4$

A pattern in rules can be seen.

1 row $p = l+1$
3 row $p = 2l+2$
5 row $p = 3l+3$
7 row $p = 4l+4$
9 row $p = 5l+5$

w rows $p = \dfrac{(w+1)l}{2} + \dfrac{(w+1)}{2}$

or $p = \tfrac{1}{2}[(w+1)l + (w+1)]$

or $p = \tfrac{1}{2}(w+1)(l+1)$

12 A 2 by 5 array is the same as a 5 by 2 array and the formula for this situation has already been worked out.

13 For 2 rows and even columns

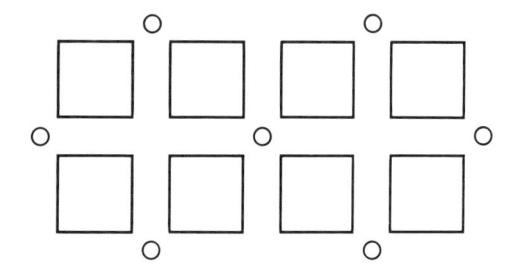

This is the optimum solution. Some pupils may work to

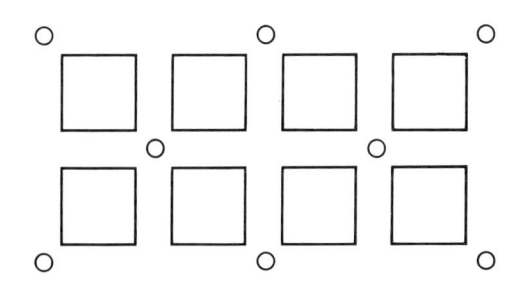

l	p
2	4
4	7
6	10
l →	$\frac{3}{2}l + 1$

14 For 4 rows and even columns

l	p
2	7
4	12
6	17
8	22
l →	$\frac{5}{2}l + 2$

For 6 rows and even columns

l	p
2	10
4	17
6	24
8	31
l →	$\frac{7}{2}l + 3$

15 Giving the pattern

2 rows $\quad p = \frac{3}{2}l + 1$
4 rows $\quad p = \frac{5}{2}l + 2$
6 rows $\quad p = \frac{7}{2}l + 3$
8 rows $\quad p = \frac{9}{2}l + 4$
w rows $\quad p = \dfrac{(w+1)l}{2} + \dfrac{w}{2}$

$\qquad\qquad\quad = \frac{1}{2}(wl + l + w)$

$\qquad\qquad\quad = \dfrac{(wl + l + w + 1 - 1)}{2}$

$\qquad\qquad\quad = \frac{1}{2}\{(w + 1)(l + 1) - 1\}$

85

Sheep dip

Anne Gorra, a mathematician from Sheepridge, decided that she would like to keep some sheep. The only problem was that she didn't have any land on which to keep them. A local farmer had a large square grass field which was not being used so it was agreed that Anne could use part of it for her sheep. The farmer lent her 24 fence panels, each one metre long, so that she could construct a pen for the sheep. The more grass the sheep had to graze on, the happier the sheep would be.

1. Show all the different arrangements of the 24 panels in the form of a rectangle that would enclose her sheep, and record your results in a table.

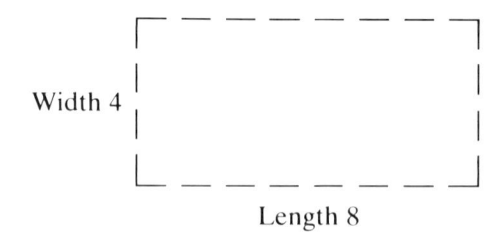

   Width 4

   Length 8

2. Which of these arrangements would make the sheep happiest? Why?

   Unhappy with this arrangement, Anne began thinking of ways of giving her sheep more room and came up with a bright idea. Why not build the rectangular pen against a wall, like this?

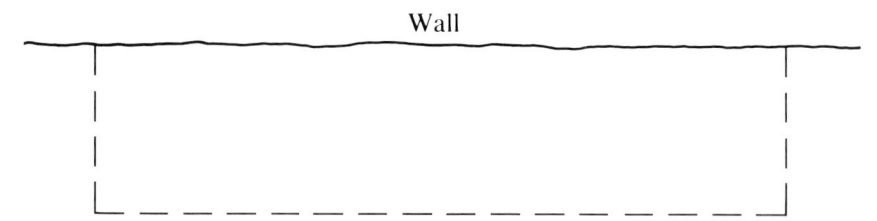

   Wall

3. Work out which arrangement of the panels against one wall would give the sheep the most grazing room.

4. There was no limit to her ingenuity and she found a way of getting 144 m² of grazing space for her sheep. How did she do this with her 24 panels?

   Later that year the farmer agreed that she could replace the 24 panels with a 24 m long electric fence.

5. If she used 4 poles to hold the fence in place in the middle of the field away from the wall, what would be the largest area that she could enclose?

6. In an attempt to make the sheep even happier she used 5 poles to hold up the fence. What is the greatest area this would now enclose?

7. Calculate the area enclosed using 6 poles, then 8 poles.

8. Work out a formula to find the area enclosed by n poles.

9. What shape should she make the fence to enclose the greatest area? What area would this be?

   Finally she reached an agreement with the farmer to enclose her sheep inside the 24 m electric fence but she was allowed to fix the fence anywhere in the field.

10. What would be the best arrangement now and in what area would the sheep have to roam around?

New York Cop and other investigations

Sheep dip

Notes

Objectives
- To develop an understanding of area optimisation given a fixed perimeter.
- To develop an ability to use trigonometry and geometry in an applied situation.

Open investigation Anne Gorra has 24 one metre fence panels in which to enclose her sheep inside a square walled grass field.

1 Which rectangular arrangement of the panels gives the sheep the most grazing room?

2 Show how you can increase this area by using the existing walls.

3 Anne decides to erect an electric fence. She has 24 metres of wire and 4 poles. What is the maximum possible grazing area for the sheep away from the wall?

4 If Anne had *n* poles and the same 24 metres of wire, what would the maximum area be?

5 What shape should she make the fence to enclose the greatest area of grass? What is this area?

6 What is the maximum possible area that can be enclosed with the 24 m electric fence and any of the existing walls? What shape is this pen?

Range of ability

	Ability	100–	80–	60–40
Age	13	5	5	5
	14	5	5	5
	15/16	Ext	10	5

Pre-knowledge
- Understanding of perimeter and area of a rectangle.
- Ability to calculate areas of regular *n* sided polygons.
- Ability to calculate circumference and area of a circle.

Equipment Matchsticks may be useful to represent fence panels.

Extensions Investigate $n \tan\left(\frac{180}{n}\right)$ for different values of *n*. What do you notice?

Solutions

1

Width	Length	Area (m²)
1	11	11
2	10	20
3	9	27
4	8	32
5	7	35
6	6	36
7	5	35
8	4	32
9	3	27
10	2	20
11	1	11

2 The 6 by 6 arrangement gives the greatest area and so gives the sheep the best grazing.

3

Width	Length	Area (m²)
1	22	22
2	20	40
3	18	54
4	16	64
5	14	70
6	12	72
7	10	70
8	8	64
9	6	54
10	4	40
11	2	22

The 6 by 12 arrangement is the best.

4 She used the corner of the field.

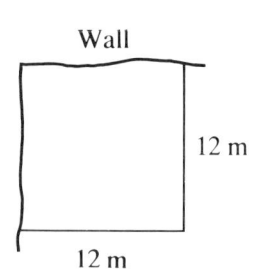

5 4 poles would give a possible area of 36 m² (see question 2).

6 5 poles would give a possible area of approx. 39.6 m².

Angle $a = \frac{360}{5} = 72$ degrees
Length $x = \frac{24}{5} = 4.8$

$2.4 = h \times \tan 36$
$h = \dfrac{2.4}{\tan 36}$
$h = 3.3$ approx

Area $= 5 \times \frac{1}{2} \times 4.8 \times 3.3 = 39.6$ m²

7 For 6 poles: a regular hexagon

angle $a = \frac{360}{6} = 60$ degrees
length $x = \frac{24}{6} = 4$
length $h = \dfrac{2}{\tan 60} = 3.5$
area of hexagon $= 6 \times \frac{1}{2} \times 4 \times 3.5 = 42$ m²

For 8 poles: a regular octagon

angle $a = \frac{360}{8} = 45$ degrees
length $x = \frac{24}{8} = 3$
length $h = \dfrac{12}{\tan 22.5} = 3.6$
area of octagon $= 8 \times \frac{1}{2} \times 3 \times 3.6 = 43.5$ m²

8 With n poles:

angle $a = \dfrac{360}{n}$
length $x = \dfrac{24}{n}$
length $h = \dfrac{12}{n \tan(180/n)}$
area $= \dfrac{144}{n \tan(180/n)}$

9 Circular area $= 45.8$ m²

10 Quadrant at the corner of the field
radius $= 15.28$ m
area $= \dfrac{733.4}{4} = 183.3$ m²

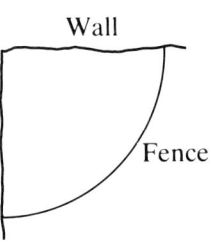

Pins in rectangles

A rectangle of length 5 units and width 4 units drawn on squared spotty paper contains 12 dots as shown in the diagram below.

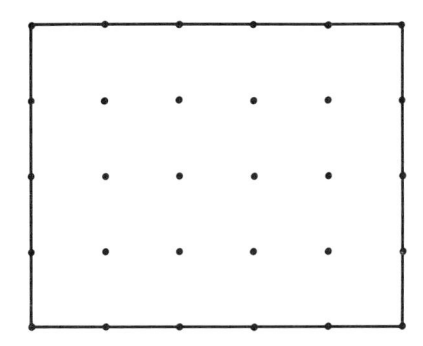

1. How many dots does a 3 by 2 rectangle contain?

2. Draw some rectangles of different sizes and see how many dots they contain.

3. Explain how you could work out the number of dots contained in any rectangle drawn on spotty paper.

4. Using l for the length and w for the width and d for the number of dots inside the rectangle write down a formula linking d, l and w.

The diagram below shows a 'diagonal rectangle' (a rectangle which is inclined at 45 degrees to the horizontal lines of dots).

This 2 by 3 diagonal rectangle contains 8 dots.

Note that the way of describing the length and width has been changed.

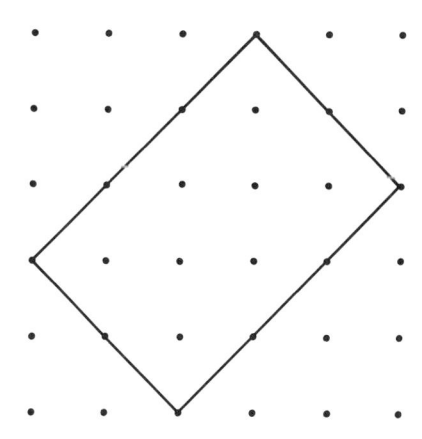

5. Draw other diagonal rectangles which have a width of 2 units. Count the number of dots inside the rectangles and record your results.

6. How many dots would a 2 by 13 diagonal rectangle contain?

7. Explain how you could work out the number of dots contained in any diagonal rectangle which has a width of 2 units.
Write a formula linking the length, l, of the rectangle and the number of dots inside, d.

8. Using diagonal rectangles of width 3 units work out a relationship between the length l and the number of dots inside, d.

9. Similarly work out relationships for rectangles of width 4 units, 5 units ...

10. Work out a formula linking the width, w, and length, l, and the number of dots, d, contained in any diagonal rectangle.

New York Cop and other investigations

Pins in rectangles

11 See if you can find relationships between the length and width of rectangles inclined at different angles to the horizontal.

This 2 by 1 rectangle contains 8 dots.

Again the unit of length has been changed.

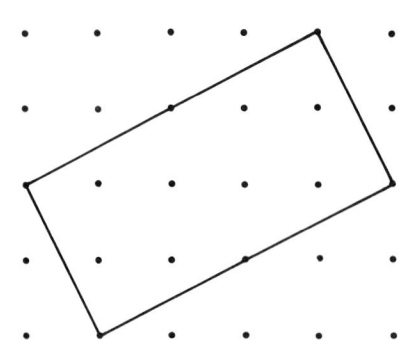

New York Cop and other investigations

Pins in rectangles

Notes

Objectives
- To develop the ability to construct three-variable formulas.
- To develop the transfer of spatial patterns into algebraic expressions.

Open investigation This rectangle, drawn on square spotty paper, has a width of 4 units and a length of 5 units. The rectangle contains 12 dots.

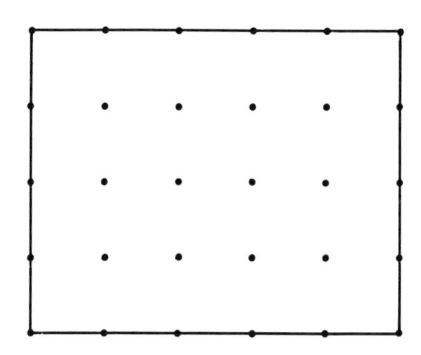

1 How many dots would a rectangle of length l and width w contain?

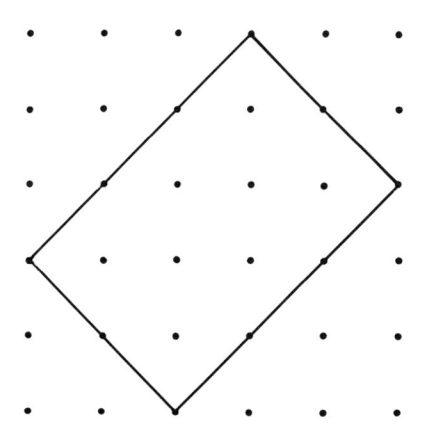

This 2 by 3 'diagonal' rectangle is inclined at an angle of 45 degrees to a line drawn across the page and contains 8 dots.

2 How many dots (d) would a diagonal rectangle of length l and width w contain?

3 Find relationships linking d, l and w for rectangles which are inclined at different angles.

Range of ability

Ability	100–	80–	60–40
Age 13	–	–	–
14	10	7	–
15/16	Ext	10	7

Pre-knowledge
- An understanding of the defining of lengths in 'units', not simply cm, m etc.
- Ability to construct simple two-variable formulas, e.g. $d = 3l - 1$ from a table of results.
- Ability to recognise three-variable formulas, e.g. $d = 2wl + 1$

Equipment Pin boards may be useful for some pupils.
A master of square spotty paper is provided at the back of this book.

Extensions This is a complete investigation in itself but other ideas are to find the number of different sized rectangles or squares that can be drawn on a 3 by 3, 4 by 4, ... dot grid.

New York Cop and other investigations

Solutions

1 2

2 See pupil's work.

3 Number of dots is (one less than the width) multiplied by (one less than the length).

4 $d = (l - 1)(w - 1)$

5
Length	Dots
1	2
2	5
3	8

6 38

7 $d = 3l - 1$

8 $d = 5l - 2$

9 4 units width $d = 7l - 3$
5 units width $d = 9l - 4$

10 $d = (2w - 1)l - (w - 1)$
$= 2wl - l - w + 1$

A possible aside is to look at diagonal squares.
1 by 1 contains 1 dot
2 by 2 contains 5 dots – $2^2 = 1^2$
3 by 3 contains 13 dots – $3^2 = 2^2$
4 by 4 contains 25 dots – $4^2 = 3^2$
m by m contains $m^2 + (m - 1)^2$

For rectangles inclined at a gradient of $\frac{1}{2}$

11
2 by 1	8	1 by 2	8	1 by 3	12
3 by 1	12	2 by 2	17	2 by 3	26
4 by 1	16	3 by 2	26	3 by 3	40
l by 1 → $4l$		4 by 2	35	4 by 3	54
		l by 2 → $9l - 1$		l by 3 → $14l - 2$	

w	d
1	$4l$
2	$9l - 1$
3	$14l - 2$
4	$19l - 3$
5	$24l - 4$

$w → (5w - 1)l - (w - 1)$
$5wl - l - w + 1$

Gradient $\frac{1}{3}$ $d = 10wl - l - w + 1$

In general for $1/g$, $d = (g^2 + 1)wl - l - w + 1$

Gradient 0 $d = wl - w - l + 1$
1 $d = 2wl - w - l + 1$
$\frac{1}{2}$ $d = 5wl - w - l + 1$
$\frac{1}{3}$ $d = 10wl - w - l + 1$
$\frac{1}{g}$ $d = (g^2 + 1)wl - w - l + 1$

$\frac{2}{3}$ $d = 13wl - w - l + 1$
$\frac{2}{5}$ $d = 29wl - w - l + 1$
$\frac{a}{b}$ $d = (a^2 + b^2)wl - w - l + 1$

Number walls

Brighouse market / New York Cop

Square spotty paper

Triangular spotty paper